THE ART OF MAKING MOJOS

How to Craft Conjure hands, Trick Bags, Tobies, Gree-Grees, Jomos, Jacks, and Nation Sacks

CATHERINE YRONWODE

Lucky Mojo Curio Company
Forestville, California

✦ 2018 ✦

The Art of Making Mojos:
How to Craft Conjure Hands, Trick Bags, Tobies, Gree-Grees,
Jomos, Jacks, and Nation Sacks
by catherine yronwode

© 2018 catherine yronwode
LuckyMojo.com/cat

Author:
catherine yronwode

Editor:
catherine yronwode

Cover:
Grey Townsend, Charles C. Dawson

Illustrations:
Grey Townsend, Charles C. Dawson, Charles M. Quinlan, Unknown Artists

Production:
nagasiva yronwode, Grey Townsend, catherine yronwode

Some material in this book appeared in draft form at these web sites:
"Hoodoo in Theory and Practice" by catherine yronwode
"Southern Spirits" by catherine yronwode
LuckyMojo.com/hoodoo.html
Southern-Spirits.com

First Edition 2018

Published by
The Lucky Mojo Curio Company
6632 Covey Road
Forestville, California 95436
LuckyMojo.com

ISBN: 978-0-9997809-0-9

Printed in Canada.

TABLE OF CONTENTS

DEDICATION

To my good friend George Ray Brown, a mighty mojo man.
and
To Liselotte F. Glozer, who taught me how to support myself.

ACKNOWLEDGEMENTS

This book could not have been written without the helpful assistance of my dear husband, nagasiva yronwode, production wrangler, proofreader, printer's liaison, and co-publisher. To you, once again, i owe so very much that it is but a small recompense to place your name at the head of the list.

To my compatriots in the world of book production, a hearty handshake and a big hug: Grey Townsend and Fred Burke — Thank you!

My thanks are also gratefully tendered to those who have patiently born with me while i was away in the type-mines, chiselling out the glimmering words and arranging them on an antique Chinese tray for purchase. To my colleagues in the Lucky Mojo Curio Co. shop — Leslie Lowell, Eileen Edler, Heidi Simpson, Ernie Medeiros, Margee Stephens, Nicole Carevich, Yosé Witmus, Jenne Nelson, and Angela Marie Horner — you have all been of help, and i thank you all.

To my students, my conjure clients, my fellow moderators and all the members of the Lucky Mojo Forum, my co-pastors in the Association of Independent Spiritual Churches, my colleagues in the Association of Independent Readers and Rootworkers, and my social friends from around the world i also extend a hand in thanks. Your companionship and good wishes keep me happy and content in my chosen line of work.

And last, but not least, i heartily acknowledge the debt i owe to the African-American originators of hoodoo and to those of any race who have documented the work. You will find some of their names in the Bibliography at the end of this book. Some i met while they were living, some i only know through books. Special thanks to Alice Bacon, Leonora Herron, Newbell Niles Puckett, Zora Neale Hurston, Jim Haskins, Rev. Jack Rondo, West Leland, Matthew Murray, Leroy "Hurky" Thomas, Larry B. Wright, Thomas "Pop" Williams, Mister Felix, Harry Middleton Hyatt, and the 1,600 rootworkers whom Hyatt interviewed between 1936 and 1970.

A HAND BY ANY NAME

MOJO, MOJO HAND, MOJO BAG

Everybody in America seems to have heard the word "mojo," but darned few White folks know what it means. Cecil Adams, author of *"The Straight Dope"* series that purports to give truthful answers to often-asked trivial questions, mumbled his way through theories that "mojo" means the sex act or a male sexual organ, even giving space to the drug-addled White singer Jim Morrison's self-applied sobriquet of "Mr. Mojo Risin'" as an indication that a mojo may be a penis. By the end of the 20th century, the second Austin Powers movie, steeped in White retro-culture, reinforced the idea of the mojo as a sex organ, but other White people took the idea in different directions, giving rise to a brand of mountain bike called a Mojo, a brand of cookies called Mojos, and numerous pets (especially cats) named "Mojo" by their loving owners.

For the record, "Mr. Mojo Risin'" is nothing more than an anagram for "Jim Morrison" and it came about because during the 1960s, Morrison apparently heard the word "mojo" on a recording by the Mississippi-born, Chicago-style blues singer Muddy Waters [McKinley Morganfield], one of whose most popular songs was called *"I Got My Mojo Working."*

How the failure of Morganfield's mojo was cast into the phantasy of a male sex organ is a tale only White musicians and newspaper columnists can unravel; after all, the first recording of *"I Got My Mojo Working"* was made by Ann Cole, a woman, and the famed Robert Johnson had sung about a woman's mojo in "Little Queen of Spades," way back in the 1930s. The truth is, the word does not refer to the sex organs of either gender and never has.

So what is a mojo? It is, in short, the staple amulet of African-American hoodoo, a packet or bag containing magical items. The word is thought by many to derive from the English word "magic." Some say it comes from the West African word "mojuba," a prayer of praise. Others derive it from the Bantu / Congo word "mooyoo," the magically-charged ashes and ground up bones of an ancestor encased in the front of a nkisi ndoki fetish-statue. This connection with the bones of the dead is interesting, because historically, many mojos have indeed contained small bones of animals or humans.

Alternative names for the mojo include hand, conjure hand, conjure bag, lucky hand, trick bag, root bag, toby, jomo, ju-ju bag, oanga, and gree-gree. In the Memphis region, a special mojo, worn only by women, is called a nation sack. A mojo used for divination is called a jack, jack bag, or jack ball.

JU-JU

In Robert H. Nassau's "Fetishism in West Africa" (1904) we learn that "the native word on the Liberian coast [for a charm bag] is 'gree-gree'; in the Niger Delta, 'ju-ju'; in the Gabun country, 'monda'; among the … Fang, 'biah'; and in other tribes the same respective [word] by which we translate 'medicine.'" Of these words, monda and biah did not make the transition to English, but ju-ju has survived, although it entered English primarily as a generalized term for "magic." It is seen in phrases like "good ju-ju" or "bad ju-ju," and it is used exactly the same way the English word "medicine" is used when one speaks of Native American "good medicine" or a "medicine man."

GREE-GREE, GRIS-GRIS, GRI-GRI, GRI-GAT

The word gree-gree made a firm transition to English. It still relates to what Nassau called the "inseparable" link between "the adjuvant medicinal herb used by the doctor, and its associated efficiency-giving spirit invoked by that same doctor." A gree-gree is a bag of herbal, magical spirit-medicine.

The spelling "gris-gris" looks French (and in French it would mean "grey-grey"), but it is simply a Frenchified spelling of gree-gree or gri-gri. Gri-gat is another variant of this word used in America. It is found in an account published anonymously in *"The Memphis Appeal"* newspaper circa 1865-1867, and quoted in full by the African-American rootworker and Spiritualist medium Paschal Beverly Randolph in his 1870 book *"Seership!"*:

"In the neighbourhood were two negroes who bore the reputation of being hoodoo men. They were both Congoes, and were a portion of the cargo of slaves that had run into Mobile Bay in 1860 or 1861. These two hoodoos were deadly enemies, and worked against each other in every possible way. Each had his own particular crowd of adherents, who believed him to be able to make the more powerful grigats."

The notation that the two hoodoo men were "Congoes" is important, for although many scholars of the 20th century considered hoodoo to be a remnant or survival from West African religions, it is quite apparent that both Jamaican obeah and United States hoodoo are primarily derived from Congo practices.

CONJURE BAG, CONJURE SACK, CONJURE HAND

The word "conjure," as in "conjure work" (casting spells) and "conjure woman" (a female herbalist-magician), is an old English alternative to "hoodoo." Thus a conjure hand is a charm bag made by a conjure doctor.

JACK, JACK BALL, LUCK BALL, GOOFER BALL

A jack ball, usually made by a professional rootworker, contains a client's personal concerns at the center and is wound around and around with a wrapping of thread, string, or yarn. The jack has several functions that the mojo does not have. It can be used as a pendulum to divine the best days or times on which to gamble or make business deals, it can be employed to determine the mental or physical health of the one for whom it was made, and it can be used to draw a person toward you or to send a person away. The bag that holds a jack ball is not a mojo bag. It is just a convenient carrying sack.

NATION SACK

The nation sack is of special interest to women, because it is used to keep a man faithful and true or to make him generous in money matters. It so happens that it is also of special interest to blues fans because it is mentioned in what may be Robert Johnson's finest song, "Come On In My Kitchen," recorded in 1936. The name seems to have originated around Memphis, Tennessee, and adjacent Mississippi and Arkansas, where Robert Johnson spent his youth. The term nation sack is probably not a shortened form for "donation sack," despite the fact that a well-known blues scholar once speculated that it was. Many people from the Memphis area also call it a nature sack — that is, one in which a man's nature is captured. The two words, nation and nature, do not mean the same thing, but may be used interchangeably.

JOMO, JOOMO, JOOMOO, JOE MOE, JOE MOW, JOE MOORE

A jomo is a lucky charm or charm bag, but its name is a bit of mystery. The common assumption is that jomo, also pronounced jomoo, joomoo, and Joe Moore, is merely a syllabic inversion of the word "mojo." This theory has led some to claim that jomo is a secret way to say mojo, so as to not arouse suspicions of performing witchcraft. But there are reasons to doubt this. For one thing, White people in America generally have no idea what a mojo is, so hiding one unknown word by using another unknown word is pointless, while Black people are already familiar with the word "jomo," thus obviating its efficacy as a cover-word. Furthermore, according to the singer Waymon "Sloppy" Henry and an elderly ex-clergyman interviewed by Harry Hyatt in the 1930s, generalized magical work is done by a "jomo man," and to "jomo work you" is the equivalent of "to rootwork you" or "to hoodoo you" — that is, to perform spells on you.

TOBY

I have no scholarly confirmation from an academic perspective, but in looking over a Bantu / Congo dictionary a number of years ago, i was struck by the fact that the word "tobé" — meaning a "tied hunting charm" — sounds like the word toby and that functionally the two are the same, in that both are tied shut and the toby is used to gain advantage, just as a hunting charm would be used. I relate this also to the old African-American term for prepared and fixed gambling money. It is called "trained hunting money," as if one were out to capture game. I may be wrong here, but if i am, it would take a very convincing argument from a linguist to shake this notion out of my head.

TRICK BAG, TRICKER BAG, TRICKEN BAG

The word trick is found in an African-American term for spell-casting — "laying tricks." To lay a trick is to do a job of work that is physically prepared and deployed somewhere to influence the life of another person. Thus, a trick bag is a bag that contains a spell, but whereas a mojo is generally made for the improvement of one's own life, a trick bag is made to contol another, and not always beneficially. Mary Alicia Owen's account of a 19th century tricker bag came from people of mixed African and Native American descent.

HAND

The word "hand" in this context means a combination of ingredients. The term may derive from the use of finger and hand bones of the dead in mojo bags, from the use of a rare Orchid called Lucky Hand Root as an ingredient, or by an analogy between the mixed ingredients in the bag and the several cards that make up a "hand" in card games.

OANGA, WANGA, OBEAH BAG

In the Caribbean, an African-derived charm bag is called a wanga or oanga bag — but that word is uncommon in the United States. If made by an obeah man (that is, a root doctor), it may be called an obeah bag.

Read more at *"Hoodoo in Theory and Practice"* and *"Southern Spirits"*:
LuckyMojo.com/mojo.html
LuckyMojo.com/jomo.html
LuckyMojo/com/nationsack.html
Southern-Spirits.com/owen-hoodoo-luck-balls.html

Mojo bags offered by mail order, 1925 - 2018. Art by Charles C. Dawson, J. C. Strong, Grey Townsend, and Unknown Artists for Oracle Products, King Novelty, Sovereign Products, J. C. Strong, Jack Daniels, E. F. Hoyt & Co., and the Lucky Mojo Curio Co.

26 BLUES LYRICS ABOUT MOJO HANDS, 1925 - 1963

Going to the Louisiana bottom to get me a hoodoo hand
Gotta stop these women from taking my man
        (*Louisiana Hoo Doo Blues,* Ma Rainey, 1925)

It must be a black cat bone, jomo can't work that hard
Every time I wake up, Jim Tampa's in my yard
        (*Jim Tampa Blues,* Lucille Bogan, 1927)

I'm going to Louisiana, to get myself a mojo hand
'Cause these backbiting women are trying to take my man
        (*Mojo Hand Blues,* Ida Cox, 1927)

Oh, the mojoe blues, Mama, crawlin' across the floor
Some hard-luck rascal told me I ain't here no more
        (*Mojoe Blues,* Charley Lincoln 1927)

I'm going to Louisiana to get me a hoodoo hand
Gonna stop you women from messing with my man
        (*Superstitious Blues,* Hattie Burleson, 1928)

My rider's got a mojo, and she won't let me see
Every time I start to lovin', she ease that thing on me
        (*Low Down Mojo Blues,* Blind Lemon Jefferson, 1928)

I'm going to Louisiana, get me a mojo hand
Just to see when my woman got another man
        (*Tell Me Woman Blues,* Texas Alexander, 1928)

Lord, I'm goin' to Louisiana, I'll get me a mojo hand
I'm gonna stop my woman an' fix her so she can't have another man
        (*Two Strings Blues,* Little Hat Jones, 1929)

Aunt Caroline Dye she told me, "Son, you don't have to live so rough;
"I'm going to fix you up a mojo, oh Lord, so you can strut your stuff"
        (*Aunt Caroline Dyer Blues,* The Memphis Jug Band, 1930)

I'm goin' to New Orleans to get this toby fixed of mine
I am havin' trouble, trouble; I can't keep from cryin'
        (*Spider's Nest Blues,* Hattie Hart and The Memphis Jug Band, 1930)

My gal got a mojo, she's tryin' to keep it hid
But Georgia Bill got something to find that mojo with
        (*Scarey Day Blues,* Blind Willie McTell, 1932)

I wear my mojo above my knee to keep you from tryin' to hoodoo me
So keep your hands off a' my mojo, if you ain't got no stuff for me
        (*Take Your Hands Off My Mojo,* "Coot" Grant and "Kid" Wilson, 1932)

You know, I let that woman tote my money, Lord, in a jomo sack
It's going to be some Hell raised, Lord, if she don't bring some of my money back
        (*Penniless Blues,* Walter Roland, 1935)

My baby, she got a mojo, tryin' to keep it hid
Papa Weaver got something, find that mojo with
    (*Fried Pie Blues,* Curley Weaver, 1935)

Oh-ah, she's gone; I know she won't come back
I've taken the last nickel out of her nation sack
    (*Come On In My Kitchen,* Robert Johnson, 1936)

Everybody say she got a mojo, 'cause she been usin' that stuff
But she got a way trimmin' down, hoo fair brown, and I mean it's most too tough
    (*Little Queen of Spades,* Robert Johnson, 1937)

'Cause I'm going to Louisiana just to get me a mojo hand
And I won't stop trying 'til I get you under my command
    (*Anna Lou Blues,* Tampa Red, 1940)

One night I'm goin' down into Louisiana and buy me another mojo hand
All because I got to break up my baby from lovin' this other man
    (*Hoodoo Hoodoo,* John Lee "Sonny Boy" Williamson, 1946)

Now, Miss Hoodoo Lady, please give me a hoodoo hand
I want to hoodoo this woman of mine; I believe she's got another man
    (*Hoodoo Lady Blues,* Arthur "Big Boy" Crudup, 1947)

I'm going down in New Orleans, hmmmh, get me a mojo hand
I'm gonna show all you good looking women, just how to treat your man
    (*Louisiana Blues,* Muddy Waters, 1950)

I got one jack, sure is crazy
My aunt forgot to teach me, just how to operate it
    (*The Mojo,* J.B. Lenoir, 1953)

Now, I'm goin' down to Louisiana an' get me a mojo hand
My little woman she done quit me for some other man
    (*Hoodoo Man Blues,* Junior Wells, 1953)

I got a mojo and don't you know?
I'm all dressed up, no place to go
    (*I Ain't Got You,* Jimmy Reed, 1955)

I got my mojo workin' but it just don't work on you
I wanna love you so bad, child, but I don't know what to do
    (*I Got My Mojo Working,* Ann Cole, 1956)

I'm goin' to Louisiana, and get me a mojo hand
I'm gonna fix my woman so she can't have no other man
    (*Mojo Hand,* Lightning Hopkins, 1960)

The way you been actin' is such a drag
You done put me in a trick-bag
    (*Trick Bag,* Earl King, 1963)

See more songs about rootwork at the "Hoodoo in Blues Lyrics" web site:
Luckymojo.com/blues.html by Catherine Yronwode

A HANDFUL OF BASIC PRINCIPLES

A MAP OF THE TERRITORY

In this chapter i am going to cover a large number of topics that will provide you with an overview of how to make a mojo. When you begin to work with the recipes in later chapters, you will want to come back to this section and review the spiritual beliefs and procedures that inform the work.

RULE-MAKING OR THE "ONE-TRUE-WAYISM"

People new to hoodoo often try to impose make-or-break rules on conjure. In their own cultures or initiatic religions they may have learned that a horseshoe "must" point in a certain direction, magic "must only" be harmless, all spells "must" rhyme, or magical goods "must only" be made by initiated clergy who have the proper spiritual "licenses" — so they naively try to force hoodoo to comply with their own rigourous make-or-break rules. They usually do not understand what they are doing because it seems so natural to them, after all, to believe that magic has rigid rules — but those of us who have worked in conjure for a long time look at them and shake our heads. Why? Why? Why don't they join US instead of forcing us to adopt their rules?

But then, after getting maybe half of them to relax their rigid rule-making, guess what? They decide that what i said was, "There are no rules in hoodoo."

No. That is not what i said either. There are rules in hoodoo — but they are African-American hoodoo rules, not the rules of other cultures or religions.

PERSONAL CONCERNS

Not all mojo hands contain personal concerns, but if you add such items to any hand in this book, i believe you will strengthen it. Traditional concerns include fingernails, toenails, head or body hair, foot skin scrapings, and body fluids such as sweat, urine, menstrual blood, or semen on a cloth or string.

With the coming of the internet, "smart" people have taken to calling these bodily adjuncts "DNA," but they are missing the point. Folk magic has its own beliefs, and dragging in modern science is not necessary. In folk magic, a fingernail (a poor source of DNA) is more valuable than the rim of a cup which may contain traces of saliva (a good source of DNA). We are looking for a physical trace, not a CSI case, and for traditional workers, the elaboration of getting the right material (ten fingernail trimmings, ten toenail trimmings, and three hairs, for example) is evidence of the spiritual artistry of our work.

COUNTING THE NUMBER OF INGREDIENTS

Some toby makers count out ingredients, and some toby makers do not.

Nothing bad will happen to you or to your mojo if you don't count the ingredients, because all that means is that you will be one among many root doctors who never count the ingredients — and they are just as traditional as those who do. Any attempt to institute some sort of "odd-numbers rule" is pointless and inauthentic in the practice of African-American conjure, but if you do count out ingredients, here are some important ideas to consider:

- Of those workers who count out their ingredients, more tend to prefer odd numbers than even numbers.
- Of those workers who prefer an odd number of ingredients, the most common numbers folks have given me over the decades are 3, 7, and 9.
- When counting ingredients, some toby makers may count magnetic sand with a lodestone as one item, or they may count a pre-made herb mix as one item instead of enumerating the number of herbs in it — and they may do this deliberately to "fudge the count" and arrive at an odd number.

HOW BIG SHOULD A MOJO BE — AND HOW FULL?

Folks new to mojo-making regularly ask, "How big?" and "How full?" I could reply, "Small enough to tuck in your bosom or carry in your pocket," but only you know how big your bosom or your pocket is.

I tend to make small, light mojos and i safety pin them in my brassiere or carry them in my belt-pouch. A very small one can be worn pinned to the inside of a long skirt or the crotch of my panties. A large one can be carried in a purse or pocketbook. If you're a flat chested woman or a slim man, you don't want some overstuffed pillow of a mojo, but if you are a tall size XXL, you can carry a very full mojo bag indeed and no one will be the wiser.

Look at the mojo at LuckyMojo.com/mojo.html — that is one of my own personal bags. It is less than half full, as you can see by the way the cloth is folded. That little red flannel bag, by the way, is the most often illegally copied image from Lucky Mojo. It has been stolen by multiple dozens of copy-cat web sites to sell their own mojos. I took that picture in 1996 with a scanner, before i had a digital camera. What is in that mojo? Well, it contains four items only and it would be impossible for those four items to completely fill a bag. My mojo is an exact copy of a mojo that i bought from a toby-maker in Oakland, California, back in the 1960s — the very first mojo i ever bought.

PETITION PAPERS, PRAYER PAPERS, SIGILS, AND SEALS

Some mojos are made of paper, not cloth or leather. Some workers put inscribed papers in every bag they make. Some never add any form of paper at all. Some add a paper as spirit leads them when making a bag. The choice is yours, and it is both a spiritual and stylistic one. Here are some types of papers:

- Name Paper(s), with or without birth date(s).
- Photograph(s), with or without name(s) and / or birth date(s).
- Petition paper(s) containing wishes, affirmations, and / or commands.
- Paper currency, either plain or written on as a form of petition paper.
- Scriptural prayers, hand-written, photocopied, or printed.
- Talismanic seals, such as those from *"The Sixth and Seventh Books of Moses"* or *"The Key of Solomon the King."*

Here's how to make a seed-packet out of a 3-inch square Post-It note:

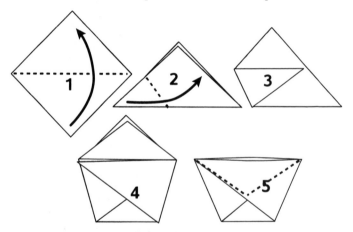

1. After you write on the paper, fold it in half on the diagonal.
2. Fold the left corner up so that its top is parallel to the bottom edge.
3. Fold the right corner up to the left, also parallel to the bottom edge.
4. Fill the envelope with herbs, powders, curios, or personal concerns.
5. Fold the two free tips into the pocket formed by the outside flap.

For more ways to prepare papers for mojo hands and other spells, see:
"Paper In My Shoe" by Catherine Yronwode

WHAT KIND OF BAG?

When it comes to a cover for your herbs, roots, curios, and talismans, you have a lot of choices. Here are the some of the most common:

- **Metal:** One of the oldest hands for which we have a list of contents was described by Mrs. L. D. Morgan in 1886. It was contained in "a spherical metal case about the size of a Goose egg, covered first with yellow, then with black leather." If you carry graveyard dirt or cremation ashes in a mojo, i recommend wrapping them in foil or putting them in a tight, non-breakable container (no plastic, no glass), and sealing the closure.
- **Paper:** Folded paper makes a nice wallet-hand, a bed-packet to slip between box springs and mattress, or a sub-container in a cloth bag.
- **Leather:** Chamois ("shammy") leather, split cowhide, and doeskin are all strong covers for a hand. Some very nice mojos are made in the scrotums of animals or by whip-stitching two leather disks together.
- **Cloth:** Red flannel is the most common cover for a roots bag, but in this book you will see brocade cloth, a crochet-edged heart-shaped packet, and a hand tied in a knot of white handkerchief. Plain cloth, fancy cloth, cloth with silk-screened artwork, and cloth bags with small charms sewn on them are authentic and time-honoured ways to make a mojo. In fact, the cloth need not be sewn — a fabric square can be wrapped and tied like a package, or drawn up around a ball-shaped bundle and tied with a string around the "neck." Flannel need not be red; since the late 1940s, folks have been colour-coding cloth to match the symbolic meanings of candle colours. And that's not all: If you are making a love mojo, you can use a piece of your lover's clothing that has been worn and not washed. The double-layer of cloth in the crotch of underwear is an excellent choice. Open one edge, fill it, and use blanket-stitching or a serger to close it up.
- **Thread or String:** A jack ball is wound up into a sphere by wrapping the ingredients around and around with thread, pearl cotton, or fine string and leaving a hanging loop so it can be used as a pendulum.

WRAPPING, SEWING, AND TYING

Every mojo should be tied, wrapped, or sewn shut— but not everyone does this the same way. A miller's knot, also known as a bag or sack knot, is my favourite way to finish a bag, but other knots will do just as well. If you sew your own packets, use a serger, or hand-sew a blanket stitch or crochet edging.

SETTING THE BAG TO WORK

Except with the nation sack, once your bag is sewn or tied, you will not take things out, or put things in, unless you mean to remake the hand.

There are many ways to set a mojo to working, including asking in the name of the Father, Son and the Holy Ghost; breathing or speaking to it before tying it; reciting Psalms from the Bible; passing it through incense smoke or candle flame; sprinkling or mouth-spraying it with whiskey; dabbing it with oil, perfume, or whiskey; or applying your sexual fluids, menstrual blood, urine, or spittle to it. None of these methods is "more authentic" than any other. They express regional variations, family traditions, and personal choices.

A SIMPLE PROCEDURE

This simple procedure does not incorporate all the possible variations used by every rootworker, but it provides one traditional way to fix a bag:

1) Inscribe and dress a small candle with oil appropriate to your cause.
2) Light an altar incense appropriate to your cause and pray your desire.
3) Work by the light of the candle and the light of the Sun or Moon. For example, by the Moon for sex with a lady of the night or for gambling, by the Sun for a true and faithful wife or for a prosperous store or shop.
4) Prepare the mojo, breathe life into it or pray over it, and tie or sew it up.
5) Feed it by dabbing, spraying, or sprinkling oil, perfume, or whiskey on it.
6) Warm the hand in the candle flame to make it eager to work.
7) Smoke the hand in the incense smoke to fix and prepare it.
8) Let the candle and incense burn out naturally; bury your ritual remains.
9) Wear and sleep with the mojo for at least seven days to attune it to you.

FEEDING THE HAND

If you adopted a kitten, it would be alive, but until you trained it and grew to know it, and it grew to enjoy your company, it wouldn't really be your cat. One way that bond is formed is by touching and petting the kitten; another is by feeding it. The mojo hand is considered to be alive, and so you will keep it near you for seven days, and after that you'll feed once a week with liquids.

You can feed your hand with oils, whiskey, or Hoyt's Cologne, or vary them. All of these are traditional mojo dressings. The choice is yours.

Some gambling mojos are fed with urine — often the urine of a male gambler's female lover — but they are only kept for one night of gaming play.

A FEW WORDS ABOUT WHISKEY

When the era of Prohibition in the USA put a halt to using whiskey to dress mojos and jacks, people began to substitute perfumes or herbal dressing oils. With the repeal of prohibition in 1935, the use of perfumed oils remained popular, but whiskey and perfumes returned to the repertoire as well.

The mojo hand recipes in this book mention "whiskey" as if it were a generic liquor, but there are deep subtleties to the brand of whiskey you will choose. In their own way, these differences are as profound as the difference between Money Drawing Oil, Lucky Hand Oil, and Love Me Oil.

Some folks choose Jack Daniel's Old No. 7 Whiskey because it has a "lucky Number 7" on it and some choose Crown Royal Whisky because it has a "Crown of Success" on it. Seagrams's 7 Crown Whiskey has both.

One man, who was half Black and half Cherokee, told me to use Wild Turkey or Old Crow Whiskey because "those are Indian names."

Some people use Johnny Walker to dress a "Three John Roots" bag for obvious reasons, to fix a jack ball because "Jack is short for John" or for a health-restorative mojo because "Johnny Walker keeps you walking."

Meanwhile, Four Roses Whiskey would recommend itself for love work, Southern Comfort for a happy home, and Old Grand-Dad might be your choice if you were working with your grandfather's graveyard dirt.

In other words, the use of whiskey to feed a mojo is old and authentic, and the liquor's brand name may represent a significant spiritual consideration.

SEEING OR TOUCHING IT KILLS THE HAND

All of the power of a toby or nation sack will be undone, and the hand itself will be killed, if a stranger, or your lover, touches it or looks inside. This is probably the strongest taboo governing the use of the mojo hand. However, a touched, seen, unfed, or ailing mojo may not be as dead as you think it is. Do a divination to see if there is any life left, then try to revive it with Grains of Paradise, as explained on page 19. It that fails, bury it, burn it, or remake it.

There are, by the way, a few exceptions to the "no touching" rule:

Couples may know about, see, or touch a mutually-made house protection mojo or a baby blessing toby. In this case, the couple functions as a single entity — but no friends or other family members should see the bag.

Additionally, shared bags for travel are often swapped. Each party holds the other's mojo while they are apart, and the hands are traded back when the couple reunites — but no one outside the dyadic couple should see either bag.

HOW FOLKS CARRY A MOJO HAND
- Most people tote or carry their mojo on their persons.
- Women like to wear them in their bras, secured by a pin or neck-string.
- Women frequently carry them in their purse rather than a pocket.
- Men often carry them in a pants pocket; a small one fits a watch pocket.
- Small protection packets can be sewn into a child's clothes or backpack.
- A mojo in a watch case won't tell time but it is "hidden in plain sight."
- Pinning a mojo in your underwear keeps your sex on your lover's mind.
- Some truck drivers and chauffeurs keep them in their glove boxes.
- They can be carried in an instrument case if you are a musician.
- They may be stashed between the box springs and mattress of your bed.
- Some folks keep their mojo in a bureau drawer while not carrying it.
- When i am on the road, i hide mine in my shoe before i go to bed.

HOW MANY PURPOSES CAN ONE MOJO HAVE?
Some folks only have one mojo, either a special purpose bag, such as a money mojo, or an all-purpose bag like our Southern Herb Bag. Some folks have several mojos at home but carry only one on their body at a time, based on where they are going or what they are doing. Some people carry two or more — and i know one man from an old-time family of conjure doctors in Baton Rouge who regularly carries three or four.

If you want to carry just one hand that is truly "all-purpose," you have a couple of choices: you can mix together a large number of herbs — one for love, one for money, one for health, and so forth — or you can select a smaller number of herbs that are known to do double or triple duty, that is, curios like John the Conqueror, which brings gambling luck, good health, and male power; and Mint, which is both protective and a money-attractor.

ROLLING THE MOJO, WORKING THE JACK
In addition to carrying a hand, some folks work, roll, or operate it. For example, in 1939, Rev. Hyatt spoke with a 28-year-old bootlegger in Waycross, Georgia, who described a jomoo made for him by a Florida root doctor to keep off the law. He said, "During the time they [the police] supposed to travel that beat, I'd just roll my jomoo and they'd pass on by. I tried it and it worked."

Likewise, a jack, in addition to bringing luck and finding use as a dowsing pendulum, may also be employed in spell-casting. By forcing it to swing to and fro as you speak to it, you can reel in a loved one or drive your enemies away.

HOW LONG DOES A MOJO LAST?

In my younger days, i asked many a toby maker how long a mojo lasts, and i received a variety of responses. These ideas came from individuals all around the country. They probably reflected local or regional styles of work.

- **First, try reviving it:** If a mojo for luck, love, or money seems to be failing in strength, try adding Grains of Paradise to it. At the same time, chew some Grains of Paradise, take whiskey into your mouth and spit a bit of the whiskey onto the mojo. This has been known to bring back a mojo that was "killed" by an enemy and to wake up a mojo that was weakened because it was left in a drawer unattended for too long. It's always worth a try before you give up on it. I call this "Revival Style."
- **Get a new one once a year or when it begins to fail:** *"It's like a haircut; you know that one haircut won't last you all your life." "Every old dog has to die sometime." "Just bury it."* I call this "Haircut Style."
- **When the cloth begins to fray or look bad:** *"That old cloth is just plumb worn out, like an old suit of clothes, but it's still working for you, so just put everything into a new cover."* I call this "Cumulative Style."
- **Keep the minerals and roots but renew the papers and herbs:** *"Bring it back and i'll fix it up for you again with a new cover."* I call this "Renewal Style." To renew a mojo, open it up and set all the hard roots, coins, stones, or bones aside. Return the soft items, including herbs, dusts, and torn or worn papers, to the bag and bury it. Wash the hard items in whiskey, Hoyt's Cologne, Florida Water, or perfume. Whiskey is traditional, all-purpose, and can be mouth-sprayed. Hoyt's Cologne is for gambling and money drawing hands. Florida Water is enjoyed by many for blessing. Various perfumes are indicated for whatever condition they are named for. Get a new flannel bag and new "soft" items. Replace any papers you want to change. Make up the bag from scratch, with prayers and the usual smoking, praying, or blowing into it, tying it, dressing it, and so forth, just as it was first made.
- **Re-Using or Rededicating Curios:** *"Can't i just re-use my lodestones for my new lover?"* I call this "Too Cheap Style." You can re-use some curios, but if i'd made a bag for love and put two lodestones in it dedicated in my and my lover's names, and i changed my mind, i would bury those lodestones, just the same as burying that love affair. I would start over with two new lodestones dedicated to myself and my new lover.

SOME WORDS OF CAUTIOUS ADVICE

I do not recommend a person who is very new to hoodoo to begin by making a mojo bag. It is not entry-level work by any means. In my opinion, if you have never seen a mojo, you are not yet ready to be making one from this book. You need to buy a few from different folks, check them out, sort through them, and develop a real, on-the-ground picture of the territory.

There is a reason that most home practitioners purchase mojo bags — and it is not laziness. When you consult with a professional toby maker and have a hand made for you, you are getting an artisanal, lovingly made, and specially prepared spiritual handicraft. In time, you too may become a handicrafter of such items in your own right but making mojos is not easy. There are many traditions to the spiritual side of the work and there are many styles, methods, and finishes to the handicraft side as well.

Since the early 20th century, mojos have been sold through the mails. More than a hundred years of this custom have made mail-order mojos a common spiritual supply. Have you ever bought a mojo from a professional maker? If not, buy at least THREE, from three different persons. Once you get them, take them apart and examine them. Then re-make them for your purposes.

Ask about the beliefs of the makers you approach. If their tradition is Wicca, Feri, Appalachian Granny-Magic, Santeria, Palo, or Voodoo, move on and try someone else. They may be adept at hoodoo, but at this point in your studies, you will not know if they are good or not.

Buy only from people at least 20 years older than you. I mean it, don't buy "study" mojo bags from kids in order to learn the tradition. They may be great, they may suck — but at your stage of the game, you don't yet know what is great and authentic or what is stupid and sucks. You want to buy from toby-makers at least 40 years old. And at least 60 years old is better.

Talk to the people who made the bags you bought to study. Ask them how they chose their ingredients, what prayers they said, what kind of knot they used, and so forth. Some will not want to tell you, especially if you are pushy or just bought one bag from them. Others may offer to train you for, say, $100.00. Do you think i did not pay these fees in my younger days? I did!

In this chapter i have shown you a number of good, traditional ways to put mojo hands together for various purposes. In the next section of this book, i will share more than 100 "recipes" you can use, as if following a cookbook. Don't try to reinvent the wheel. Study and learn, make a few bags according to well-known ways, and then you will be ready to design your own hands.

THE HAND OF ABUNDANCE

CARRYING A MOJO FOR MONEY

The most popular type of mojo, far and away, is the lucky mojo — the hand that brings money, good times, a winning edge, and all-around prosperity to gamblers, business people, and those who work for a living.

In this chapter you will find traditional mojo hands that are said to:

- **Bring general good luck.**
- **Draw money through business ventures.**
- **Attract money through gifts and inheritances.**
- **Help you retain your money by preserving what you have.**
- **Help you find and keep a job.**
- **Assist you to successfully ask for a raise or promotion on the job.**
- **Assist you to get a loan or an extension on a loan repayment.**
- **Help you to have and to remember lucky dreams for gambling.**
- **Give you a winning edge in games of chance.**
- **Increase your chances of hitting when you play the lottery.**

MINERALS FOR MONEY DRAWING

Here is a list of minerals included in the money mojos in this chapter:

- **Alum:** A protective mineral to shut the mouths of gossippers and foes.
- **Baking Soda:** To make your money "rise" or "grow" as you gamble.
- **Blueing Balls:** Protective; invites good spirits; cleanses; brings peace.
- **Coins of Various Types:** Symbols of wealth, especially the silver dime.
- **Crossroads Sand:** For attraction and dispersal to the ends of the Earth.
- **Graveyard Dirt:** To engage the help of a kindly or familial spirit.
- **Gunpowder:** To speed up events and break through blockages.
- **Lodestone and Magnetic Sand:** To draw and attract what you want.
- **Needles:** Steel; attracted to a strong lodestone to prove its power.
- **Pyrite:** A symbol of wealth due to its golden-tone colour and sparkle.
- **Salt:** A protective and helpful mineral, it stabilizes and preserves things.
- **Saltpeter:** An ingredient in gunpowder, it excites money matters.

HERBS AND ROOTS FOR MONEY DRAWING

These are the herbs, roots, and zoological curios used in money mojos:

- **Abrus (Crab Eye) and Ormosia (Huayruru) Beans:** For good luck.
- **Adam and Eve Roots:** Male and female power; endangered species.
- **Agrimony:** To reverse a jinx, curse, or hex on your money or luck.
- **Alfalfa:** To protect against poverty; to get a loan; for money-luck.
- **Alkanet:** Stops those who want your money or jinx your gambling luck.
- **Alligator Foot and Tooth:** For good luck getting and holding money.
- **Allspice:** For prosperity, success, luck, and money through business.
- **Angelica Root:** Angelic help; female magical power and strength.
- **Badger Tooth:** A rare but highly traditional gambling luck curio.
- **Balm of Gilead Buds:** An acceptable substitute for Adam and Eve Roots.
- **Bat, Bat Nut, Bullbat Feather:** For powerful gambling luck.
- **Bayberry Root:** To attract more money and good fortune to you.
- **Black-Eyed Peas:** For money-luck, especially at the New Year.
- **Black Cat Hair:** For reverse bad luck; to win in games of chance.
- **Black Snake Root:** Provides magical protection; energizes the timid.
- **Blood Root:** For male and female or family power; brings respect.
- **Blue Flag:** For prosperity, and to bring in wealth and abundance.
- **Bo' Hog (Lovage) Root:** For luck in love, passion, and sexuality.
- **Buckeye:** For good luck, good health, and to enhance male vigour.
- **Calamus Root:** To control a situation or to dominate a person.
- **Cat's Eye Shells:** Repels the evil eye if carried or worn on the body.
- **Chamomile:** To bring luck in money and games of chance.
- **Cinnamon:** To rapidly attract luck, money, love, and protection.
- **Cloves:** To attract good luck to your home; to sustain friendships.
- **Dandelion Root:** To enhance psychic dreams for luck in betting.
- **Deer's Eye (Ojo de Venado) Beans:** Protects against the evil eye.
- **Devil's Shoe Strings:** For gambling luck, job getting, and protection.
- **Dragon's Blood Resin:** For good luck and invocations to spirits.
- **Fenugreek Seed:** For prosperity, increase in wages, lucky money.
- **Five Finger Grass:** For all that five fingers can do; to get favours.
- **Gentian Root:** For lucky money gained through love and romance.
- **Ginger Root:** For protection from evil magic; to heat up good luck.
- **Ginseng Root:** For male vigour and nature; good luck in gambling.

- **Grains of Paradise:** For luck, protection, and wishes; to get a job.
- **Gravel Root:** For a new job or when asking for a raise or benefits.
- **Irish Moss:** For a steady flow of money in business and gambling.
- **Job's Tears Seeds:** To be granted an important wish in money or love.
- **John the Conqueror Root:** For personal power, gambling, money luck.
- **Lemon Grass:** For protection; to increase the power of all amulets.
- **Little John to Chew Root:** To overcome legal and social troubles.
- **Lucky Hand Root:** To increase gambling luck through dexterity.
- **Lucky Rock (Fish Ear Bone):** For luck, business, job-getting, money.
- **Mace:** To draw money through games of chance or a business venture.
- **Master Root:** For protection, psychism, and luck; to command respect.
- **Mint:** To break spells and jinxes; to gain mental strength and insight.
- **Mojo Beans:** For good luck and wealth; to make wishes come true.
- **Nutmeg:** A powerful lucky charm to bring in gambler's winnings.
- **Patchouli:** For love-drawing and money-drawing, and to break jinxes.
- **Peony Root:** To protect, aid health, break jinxes, and draw good luck.
- **Quassia:** For controlling and domination, such as when gambling.
- **Queen Elizabeth Root:** Grants the power of attraction to women.
- **Rabbit Foot:** For all-around good luck in money, love, and games.
- **Raccoon Penis Bone or Baculum:** Good luck and steady money wins.
- **Rattlesnake Master:** For protection from "snakes in the grass."
- **Red Pepper:** For protection from enemies; for cleaning away evil.
- **Rose Hips:** For love and protection of health, family, and the home.
- **Rue:** To break curses, hexes, or jinxes; to ward off the evil eye.
- **Sampson Snake Root:** To give power and strength, especially to men.
- **Sandalwood:** For love, health, and money drawing; to protect from evil.
- **Sarsaparilla:** For health and sex; to draw money; to bless a house.
- **Sassafras:** To help you control and make your money go further.
- **Sea Beans and Sea Heart Beans:** For good luck and protection.
- **Smart Weed:** For luck and money; protects against friendly enemies.
- **Snake Skin Sheds:** To protect from snake bite and sweet deceivers.
- **Snake Weed:** For luck; to protect against snakes and false friends.
- **Southern (Dixie) John Root:** For a happy home life and good luck.
- **Thyme:** To make money grow and stay with you; for good health.
- **Tobacco Snuff:** An herb of power for reaching into the spirit world.
- **Tonka Beans:** To make love-wishes come true; for money in love.
- **White Snake Root (Boneset):** To break jinxes and ward off snakes.

DRESSING AND FEEDING A MONEY MOJO

- **Algiers Oil:** A Fast Luck type formula from Algiers, Louisiana.
- **Attraction Oil:** To attract money, love, luck, success, or your desire.
- **Aunt Sally's Lucky Dream Oil:** To recollect lucky number dreams.
- **Black Cat Oil:** Used as a form of "reverse bad luck" among gamblers.
- **Boss Fix Oil:** To bring your boss around to favour your cause.
- **Crown of Success Oil:** For financial, betting, school, or career success.
- **Dragon's Blood Oil:** For luck, protection, and sealing a pact or promise.
- **Fast Luck Oil:** To bring luck in a hurry in money, love, and business.
- **Five Finger Grass Oil:** For all the things that your five fingers can do.
- **Good Luck Oil:** To give all-around luck in love, money, and business.
- **Hoyt's Cologne:** The most lucky of all perfumes for money or love.
- **John the Conqueror Oil:** For personal power, mastery, and money.
- **Lady Luck Oil:** For gamblers and those who take serious risks in life.
- **Lodestone Oil:** To draw love, luck, and money with live magnetism.
- **Lucky Buddha Oil:** To attract luck and wealth with the help of Hotei.
- **Lucky Hand Oil:** For gamblers, who say it brings in the winnings.
- **Lucky Mojo Oil:** An all-purpose lucky combination for gamblers.
- **Lucky Number Oil:** For catching lucky numbers to bet and win.
- **Lucky 13 Oil:** For lottery and bingo play; bad luck brings good luck.
- **Magnet Oil:** To attract things to you the way that magnets draw iron.
- **Mandrake Oil:** Used to draw both love and money as you wish.
- **Money Drawing Oil:** To draw money in gambling and in business.
- **Money House Blessing Oil:** For a prosperous, happy, blessed home.
- **Money Stay With Me Oil:** To see how much you can hold on to.
- **Pay Me Oil:** To get back money that is owed, by people or casinos.
- **Prosperity Oil:** To increase your income and lead you to a better life.
- **Spanish Moss Oil:** Used for wealth, and also in spiritual "war" work.
- **Special Dice Oil:** For good luck when shooting dice or playing craps.
- **Special Oil No. 20:** An all-purpose anointing oil for luck and love.
- **Steady Work Oil:** For gaining and maintaining regular employment.
- **Three Jacks And A King Oil:** For play at cards and games of chance.
- **Van Van Oil:** For opening the way; to change bad luck to good luck.
- **Victory Oil:** Used when seeking triumph over rivals or enemies.
- **Wealthy Way Oil:** For prosperity, plenitude, luxury, and an easy life.
- **Whiskey:** Jack Daniel's Old No. 7, Crown Royal, Seagrams's 7 Crown.

THE LUCKY HAND

ALL-AROUND GOOD LUCK HAND

Tobacco Snuff, John the Conqueror Root, Black Cat hair, Cat's Eye Shells, and lodestone, placed in a red bag and dressed with Black Cat Oil makes a strong mojo hand.

A SEVEN-WAY ROOT BAG FOR A MAN'S LUCK

A very strong mojo for male luck and power is made only with roots and no green herbs, contains a small piece each of Peony Root, High John the Conqueror Root, Lucky Hand Root, Bo' Hog Root, Sampson Snake Root, Master Root, and Black Snake Root. The seven roots are sewn into a brown leather bag which may be carried on one's person or hidden in the home or place of business.

A SEVEN-WAY ROOT BAG FOR A WOMAN'S LUCK

A very strong mojo for female luck and power, made only with roots and no green herbs, contains one piece each of Peony root, Queen Elizabeth Root, Lucky Hand Root, Angelica Root, Gentian root, Calamus root, and Blood Root. The seven roots are sewn into a brown leather bag which may be carried on one's person or hidden in the home or place of business.

LUCKY BEANS IN MOJO HANDS

Mojo Beans are often treated in the same way as other large brown botanical curios like Buckeye, Nutmeg, and High John the Conqueror — that is, they are oiled and carried in the pocket as a lucky piece or combined with other curios in a mojo bag or conjure hand. Deer's Eye Beans, Sea Hearts, and Sea Beans are handled in this way, and in addition to general good luck and gambling luck, the latter two, being sea-borne seeds, are also said to protect from death by drowning. Small red beans — especially *Abrus* and *Ormosia spp.* — are included in mojo bags for luck as well.

GENERAL PURPOSE LUCKY HAND

A very good general-purpose love-and-money-drawing mojo can be made with Dragon's Blood, Cinnamon chips, and three Tonka Beans. Add any other ingredients as desired, and dress the bag with Fast Luck Oil.

THREE JOHNS TRIO HAND FOR LUCK

John the Conqueror, Little John to Chew, and Southern John Root, can be combined to make a famous trio hand for the Three Johns. Pray over each root separately: Psalms 23 *("The Lord is My Shepherd...")* over the John the Conqueror, Psalms 37 *("Fret not thyself because of evildoers...")* over the Little John, and Psalms 136 *("O give thanks unto the Lord; for he is good...")* over the Southern John. Then carry them in a bag and dress the bag with Hoyt's Cologne. If you wish, this trio can also be made with chips of the roots, hair of the person, and the person's name on paper; then wrapped and wound in red thread to make a jack ball for divination as well as luck.

CROSSROADS SAND AND GRAVEYARD DIRT LUCKY JOMO

Rev. Harry Middleton Hyatt recorded this simple lucky jomo from a person known as Informant #1095 in Waycross, Georgia, in 1939: "[Go] to the forks of the road about twelve or one o'clock in the night and get some sand and put it in a bag and put it over your mantlepiece. Go to the graveyard and get some dirt and sew it up with that. And that would make you lucky — good a jomo as you'd want."

A LUCKY WISH-GRANTING MOJO

Write your secret desire on paper and cross it with your name written three times. Fold the name-paper toward you around a small, whole Dandelion root. Dress it with Holy Oil and carry it in a red bag with three Mojo Beans and seven Job's Tears, to aid in wish-fulfillment.

A RABBIT FOOT MOJO FOR LUCK, LOVE, AND MONEY

A Rabbit Foot for luck, a small Nutmeg for money, and three Tonka Beans for love will make a very strong, naturally sweet-smelling, and all-purpose luck-drawing trio. Carry them in a red flannel bag and dress the bag with Fast Luck Oil.

TO DRAW MONEY THROUGH LUCK

Make a mojo in a green bag with a Yellow Dock Root, Bayberry chips, and Cinnamon chips. The scent of pine is believed to attract money, so dress it with Pine Oil or Pine Cologne, to draw money through luck. Two good perfumes with this scent are Pino Silvestre and Polo by Ralph Lauren.

THE GAMBLER'S HAND

LUCKY STONE GAMBLING MOJO

This is my version of a gambler's hand that Rev. Hyatt was taught in 1938 by Informant #958, a rootworker in Memphis, Tennessee. Cut out two small, circular disks of chamois leather and whip-stitch them together half-way. Sandwich a silver dime between a pair of lucky rocks (fish ear bones, Drumfish otoliths). Fill in and surround them with softened Lakshmi Dhoop incense into which you have embedded Grains of Paradise. Whip-stitch the mojo tight and dress the leather cover with Double Luck Perfume Oil. Keep it oiled and fed, and wear it in your pocket for gambling luck.

ALLIGATOR FOOT CHARM OR MOJO FOR GAMBLING

The Alligator foot may be used as a key-chain fob or pocket piece and fed with whiskey, urine, Hoyt's Cologne, or Van Van Oil. To make a lucky hand, combine the foot with a whole Nutmeg, Allspice berries, Cinnamon chips, Bayberry chips, and a High John the Conqueror Root, and carry it in a red flannel bag with a paper bearing your money wishes written in red ink.

ALFALFA HAND TO MAKE YOUR STAKE LAST LONGER

Gamblers carry a pinch of Alfalfa leaves in a green flannel bag when they go to place a bet, because they believe that it will bring in money to make their stake last longer. Such a hand usually contains at least three ingredients, so the other two may be selected from among the many gambling luck curios, such as Allspice berries, Nutmeg, a Rabbit foot, or a silver dime.

A LUCKY ALLIGATOR TOOTH GAMBLING MOJO

Embed three Crab's Eye Beans with red wax in the hollows of three large Alligator teeth, To these prepared teeth, add three Mojo Beans and three Black-eyed Peas, The whole is folded and sewn into a piece of red flannel to pad and protect it, fed with Hoyt's Cologne, and carried in a leather bag.

A "TRIPLE HAND" FOR CARD-PLAYERS

Combine Five Finger Grass, Lucky Hand Root, and an Alligator foot to aid in "all the skills that five fingers can perform." Add your own fingernail clippings or those of someone who wins big. Put everything in a red flannel bag dressed with Three Jacks and a King Oil and fed with Hoyt's Cologne.

A TRADITIONAL GAMBLING HAND

A powerful gambling mojo consists of a silver Mercury dime, a small John the Conqueror Root or root chip, and a Lucky Hand Root, wrapped and folded in a two-dollar bill on which you have written your own name seven times. The folded packet is carried in a red bag dressed with Fast Luck, Three Jacks And A King, Van Van, or Bayberry Oil.

DRAGON'S BLOOD RESIN MOJO HAND FOR MONEY LUCK

A chunk of Dragon's Blood Resin is lucky for money or gambling if carried in a green flannel bag with John the Conqueror Root and a small piece of lodestone. Dress the bag with Money Drawing or Lady Luck Oil.

A LUCKY MINERAL HAND

A piece of lodestone, a piece of pyrite, and a pinch of saltpeter carried together in a red flannel bag dressed with Hoyt's Cologne makes a good all-mineral mojo hand for luck in gambling.

NINE DIMES GAMBLING MOJO

A blueing ball, a lump of rock alum, and nine silver Mercury dimes sewn up together in a red flannel bag is a good gaming charm.

AN OLD-TIME MOJO FOR GAMBLING LUCK

Another traditional conjure hand for playing games of chance contains a silver dime, a Rabbit foot, and nine short lengths of Devil's Shoe Strings roots which have been tightly rolled up and tied inside a dollar bill on which you have written your name. The three ingredients are carried in a red flannel bag dressed with the urine or menstrual blood of the gambler's beloved.

A SOVEREIGN GAMBLER'S CHARM

In *"The Long Lost Friend"* it is claimed that those who wear or carry a Badger tooth will win at gambling games such as the lottery, cards, slots, bingo, and horse-racing. The tooth can be fitted out as a watch or keychain fob, but it is safer if carried in a mojo bag with other gambler's curios. Some say that an Alligator tooth gives equally good results. Those who carry such a tooth anoint or feed it with Van Van Oil or Hoyt's Cologne and often recite the 23rd Psalm while concentrating on their desires.

A JOMO FOR GAMBLING IN NORTH CAROLINA

In 1939, Rev. Hyatt interviewed a professional worker in Fayetteville, North Carolina, whom he called Informant #1450. This man described how he made gambling jomos for his clients: At midnight take fresh, new graveyard dirt from the breast of the grave of a man who was not a Christian, but "a real gambler or some wicked man." Bring it home, add nine drops of Apple cider vinegar and a pinch of sulphur. Wrap and tie it in a piece of paper until it dries, then rub it to powder. This powder is used to fix up a "joomoo" for a client by sprinkling it onto a piece of John the Conquer Root, a piece of lodestone, and a pair of Adam and Eve Roots. (Because Adam and Eve Root is an endangered species of Orchid, i recommend you substitute a pair of Balm of Gilead Buds.) Sew everything into a red flannel bag. The worker explained that this will be a successful gambling hand as long as for every $500.00 won, the user gives $5.00 to an indigent old person.

OLD-TIME GAMBLING CHARMS

A Bat heart, a whole dried Bat, a Bat wing, the wing-feathers of a Bullbat or Nighthawk bird, or a drop of Bat blood kept in a vial of perfume are all considered lucky for gambling, especially when wrapped in red flannel or red silk and tied to the upper arm, or carried in a mojo that is slung under the arm-pit. Use Bat Nuts instead, since Bats are endangered.

PAY THIRTY PENNIES FOR A BEGGAR'S DIRT

(from *"Cash Box Conjure"* by Miss Phœnix LeFæ)

In 1939, when Rev. Hyatt was in Sumter, South Carolina, he met "The Courtroom Specialist," a middle-aged rootworker. This is his gambling hand: "Pay 30 pennies for dirt from a beggar's grave, head, chest, and foot. Buy a packet of needles and wrap three of them, two long and one short, with red thread into a cross shape. Sew the needles and a pinch of dirt in chamois." He made and sold these mojos for 50 cents each, back in the day.

A GAMBLER'S LUCKY HAND

Fix a mojo bag (red flannel for success or green flannel for money) with a Lucky Hand Root, a pinch of Five Finger Grass, a miniature pair of dice, and a John the Conqueror Root. Add either a dried Bat heart, an Alligator tooth, a Badger tooth, an Alligator Foot, or a Rabbit foot. Anoint with red Fast Luck Oil, John the Conqueror Oil, or with the urine of your lover.

MISS PHŒNIX'S FAVOURITE GAMBLING MOJO

"Burn Gambler's Gold herbs on charcoal as you put a Lucky Hand root, a High John the Conqueror Root, a Mercury dime, a whole Nutmeg, and a pinch each of Five Finger Grass and Cinnamon chips in a green bag. Make a name-paper and all over it write words like *'winner,' 'big money,' 'jackpot,'* and *'beat the house.'* Put the paper in the bag, whisper your wish, and tie the string. Feed it whiskey and Lucky Mojo Oil, and smoke it."

CRAP-SHOOTERS' MOJO WITH LUCKY DICE

A fine gambling hand is made with a pair of lucky dice that have been "retired" from play, and a pinch each of Five Finger Grass, Cinnamon, Irish Moss, Thyme, and Cloves in a red flannel bag. Dress the bag with Lady Luck Oil, Special Dice Oil, or Hoyt's Cologne.

GAMBLING HERBS AND PERFUME FOR LONGER PLAY

To keep your stake from running out, soak the money-holding herbs Irish Moss, Alfalfa, and Thyme in Hoyt's Cologne, combine these herbs with any lucky roots in a green flannel bag, and dress the bag with the fixed cologne.

THE NUTMEG OR BUCKEYE GAMBLER'S CHARM

Folks used to drill a hole in a Nutmeg or a Buckeye, fill the hole with liquid mercury, and seal it with wax as a gambling charm. Mercury is toxic and can cause nerve damage, so today's wiser workers saw a whole Nutmeg in two, sandwich a silver Mercury dime between the two pieces, and wind the whole up in red thread to make a jack ball that brings in the winnings.

LODESTONE, BAKING SODA, AND HIGH JOHN TOBY

In 1940 in Algiers, Louisiana, Informant #1592 told Rev. Hyatt, "If you want to make a hand, you can make a hand for a fellow to carry in his pocket or, if he wants, to wear it around his neck. You get you a piece of John the Conker vine. That's used often in a lot of these cases. You take you some soda, cooking [baking] soda, and you take you some lodestone, a she and a he [pair], and sew that together. Don't have to take a great big piece — just a small piece. You sew that up. You wet it with oil of Clove. You buy you some oil of Clove and you wet it. That brings luck. You buy you a bottle of Jockey Club Perfume to wash and scrub your hands. With that toby you bound to win." Why baking soda? Well, it makes your money "rise."

OLD-TIME WONDER OF THE WORLD GAMBLING HAND

Get a piece of Ginseng Root (also called Wonder of the World Root), a piece of Black Snake Root, a small John the Conqueror Root or a slice of root, and three fresh seeds from a green (unripe) Red Pepper. Fold it toward you into a scrap of red flannel, soak it thoroughly in Hoyt's Cologne, sew it up, and carry it in a red flannel bag.

SEVEN-WAY GAMBLER'S MOJO

Place a Buckeye in a green flannel bag with a silver dime, a small pair of dice, and a Rabbit foot, plus any three available money herbs, such as Alfalfa, Irish Moss, Cinnamon, Allspice, Chamomile, or Bayberry. This makes for seven ingredients, with the dice counting as one item. Dress the bag with Hoyt's Cologne. Because this hand includes dice and has seven lucky ingredients, it is popular with those who shoot dice or play casino craps.

BLACK CAT HAIR HAND FOR GAMBLING LUCK

Black Cat hair is said to bring powerful luck in games of chance when it is mixed with Patchouli and Tobacco in a mojo hand. Dress the bag with whiskey or Black Cat Oil.

A "HOT" TRIO GAMBLING HAND WITH GINGER ROOT

One toby-maker used to sell what he called a "Trio-Hand" in a red flannel bag. It consisted of a whole dried Ginger Root, a whole John the Conqueror Root, and a whole Nutmeg. Each curio had been separately prayed over with the 23rd Psalm as it was anointed with Fast Luck Oil. The assembled "trio" was then held in the hand and prayed over collectively for the desired purpose, *"In the name of God the Father, God the Son, and God the Holy Ghost,"* before being placed in the bag. The maker claimed that this was a very "hot" gambling hand — highly powerful while the spell was on, but not to be relied upon over the long haul. It could be revived by taking out the three curios and repeating the sequence of prayers and the oil-anointing process, whenever its special help was needed.

MEXICAN JOB'S TEARS HAND FOR GAMBLING LUCK

Mexican gamblers carry seven Job's Tears and a Cross of Caravaca talisman in a bag dressed with Holy Oil for luck at the lottery. This is good for seven bets, or for seven days of betting, depending on whom you ask.

RACCOON BONE FOR GAMBLING LUCK

Wrap a soft, old twenty-dollar bill around a Raccoon penis bone dressed with Hoyt's Cologne, wind it very tight with red thread, and carry it in your pocket while at play.

DR. SIMS' GUINEA GRAINS GAMBLING HAND

(from *"Cash Box Conjure"* by Miss Phœnix LeFæ)

In 1937, Rev. Hyatt met Doctor Sims, a conjure professional from New Orleans who was working in the District of Columbia at the time. A Spiritual Church minister, he taught his pupils to study the Bible, and when they passed their exams, he got them certificates of ordination from Saint John's Temple, an institution which, he said, had more White members than Black ones. He explained his gambling hand to Hyatt as a fellow academic might:

"In gambling, we say you can take a little piece of High John the Conker, you take three Guinea Grain seeds, you take a piece of lodestone, you take magic sand, and you sew these in a piece of cloth. Upon your hands you would use Oil of Van Van. Then you would hold this lucky charm in your hand whilst you are playing with a piece of money and you will be lucky."

"What is magic sand?" asked Hyatt.

"Magic sand is a thing that is made to go with this lodestone. It looks like black dust, but it comes with lodestone. You buy lodestone and they give you this sand with it," said Doctor Sims, perfectly describing magnetic sand.

ODD-NUMBERED MOJO: YOUR MONEY RETURNS TO YOU

In New Orleans, Louisiana, in 1940, Rev. Hyatt learned this trick from Informant #1560: "For luck in gambling you use the John the Conker. You take that and you can put it in a bag and you put you a little steel dust in there and put you 45 cents — two dimes and a 25 cents piece, nothing with even money, see, and put that in a bag and wear it in your pocket. And you take any high smelling perfume and you anoint it with that perfume. It seems like you would give a [rival] man ambition, when you give him those silver [coins from your mojo], and when he bet, he bet always right until the other fellow that is playing with you [a confederate] — understand, he beats him so many times until he lose ambition, see. And he be a certain amount loser thataway and he will always play. When he first start losing, he plays to win; when he find out he's losing, he plays to catch back. And [your partner] gets so far around the fellow, he beat him so much, until he just loses all ambition."

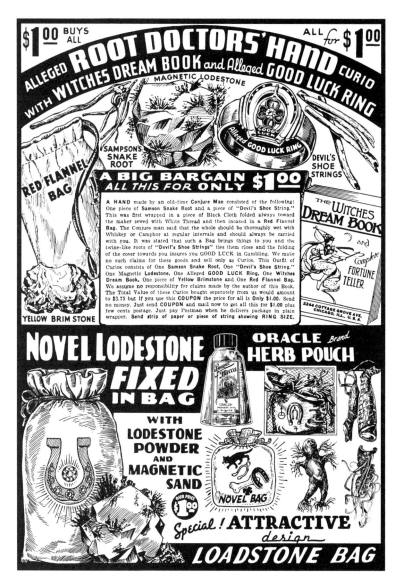

Mojo bags and curios offered in mail order hoodoo catalogues, 1925 - 2018. Art by Charles C. Dawson, Charles M. Quinlan, Grey Townsend, and One Unknown Artist for King Novelty, Sovereign Products, Oracle Products, and the Lucky Mojo Curio Co.

HANDS FOR LUCKY DREAMS

AN AID IN THE PERCEPTION OF PSYCHIC PHENOMENA
For the inducement of spiritual trances and the promotion of prophetic visions of the future, some folks make up a mojo with Anise seed, Althæa, Acacia, Calendula, Celery seed, Myrrh, and Star Anise and keep it beneath the pillow where they sleep.

A PSYCHIC VISION MOJO
To aid in the perception of psychic phenomena and promote spiritual visions, mix Celery seed, Anise seed, Althæa, Acacia, Poppy flowers, Calendula, and Star Anise in a muslin bag, and keep it in your pillow.

A SPIRITUAL CONJURE HAND FOR DIVINATION
Bearberry leaves, Anise seed, and Star Anise in combination make a mojo said to bring visionary dreams and aid divination.

FOR GOOD DREAMS AND TO STAVE OFF NIGHTMARES
Sew Rosemary and Hops into a pillow packet to ward off nightmares. Some find the smell of Lavender too strong, but if you like it, do add it.

A PILLOW PACKET TO DREAM LUCKY NUMBERS
Place a green flannel bag filled with golden Calendula flowers, Hops Flowers, Star Anise seeds, and Poppy flower petals beneath your pillow when going to sleep, because it is said that breathing the fragrance of these flowers causes one to dream of winning numbers and winning names.

FOR GREAT PERSONAL WISDOM AND LUCKY OMENS
Mix Verbena, Sage, Bay leaves, Peach Tree leaves, and Solomon Seal Root. Crumble the mix and pack some into a bottle of King Solomon Wisdom Oil. Use the rest to make one or more mojos. For each one, make a paper on which you write Proverbs 3:13 *("Happy is the man that findeth wisdom ...")* and Proverbs 4:5-9 *("Get wisdom, get understanding ...")*. Put a sprinkle of the herb mix into the paper and fold it like a seed packet. Make as many of these as you want. After seven days, the oil is ready to use to dress your forehead or hair. These packets will cause you to dream lucky and to interpret omens that will be useful when betting or making investments.

BUSINESS PROSPERITY MOJOS

A NUTMEG MONEY MOJO FOR YOUR CASH BOX
Place a whole Nutmeg in a green flannel bag with three silver dimes, and the three money herbs Allspice, Cinnamon, and Irish Moss, for a total of seven items. Keep is in your cash box. Before handling your cash, dress the bag with Money Drawing Oil and recite the 23rd Psalm. Other herbs you could use, if you wish, would be Bayberry, Thyme, Chamomile, Sassafras, Cinnamon, or Allspice — or you could just use the Nutmeg, the three dimes, and add a good-sized pinch of Besamim Lucky Money Herbs.

A MONEY-DRAWING HAND MADE WITH MOJO BEANS
Name three Mojo Beans Faith, Hope, and Charity, then pray on them in the three highest names: the Father, Son, and Holy Spirit. Put them in a square of red flannel and add Grains of Paradise and Fenugreek Seeds. Tie the hand into a little ball and dress it with a combination of Money Drawing, Money Stay With Me, and Prosperity Oil for better business. Carry it or keep it in your shop.

ATTRACTION, MONEY DRAWING, AND PROSPERITY MOJO
Place three short Cinnamon sticks dressed with Fast Luck Oil in a green bag with a John the Conqueror Root dressed with Money Drawing Oil, plus a Calamus root dressed with Attraction Oil. Dress the bag with Hoyt's Cologne. Use a few drops of the oils in your office or shop floor wash weekly.

A LUCKY HAND MOJO FOR A HANDICRAFT BUSINESS
If your business requires that you perform hand-work, dress a Lucky Hand Root, a John the Conqueror Root, and a Master Root with Lucky Hand Oil. Put them into a chamois skin bag with any of the following herbs: Allspice berries, Chamomile, Bayberry, Irish Moss, Thyme, Mint, Alfalfa, Cinnamon, or Gall of the Earth. This will not only draw money, it will protect your hands. Pray the 23rd Psalm and use the oil on the bag.

THYME IS ON YOUR SIDE
Plant Thyme in the garden, and as it grows, your money will increase. Pick some of the Thyme and dry it, then fold a dollar bill around to make a packet, tie it up, and bury it in the middle of a crossroads at the Full Moon.

GUNPOWDER AND GRAINS OF PARADISE MOJO
(from *"Cash Box Conjure"* by Miss Phœnix LeFæ)
On Rev. Hyatt's second trip to Memphis, Tennessee, in 1939, he met Informant #1541 and got this mojo recipe: "Well, you take gunpowder and lodestone and nine seeds of Red Pepper, and sew it up in a rag. That's for to draw luck to you, for money. You know, if you's a gambler, why, you can win, and if you're a policy player, why, you win like that. Or if you a business man, why, you know, your business will be more urgent [livelier]."

HIGH JOHN AND DEVIL'S SHOE STRING MOJO HAND
Wrap a John the Conqueror Root, nine small pieces of Devil's Shoe Strings Root and a silver Mercury dime in a two-dollar bill, folding the bill toward you, not away from you. If the Dime and the bill bear leap-year dates, so much the better. Fix in a red (some say green) flannel bag and anoint with Van Van Oil, John the Conqueror Oil, Hoyt's Cologne, or Prosperity Oil. This mojo draws money, boosts personal power, and enhances charisma. Wear it when playing the lottery or betting on horses, or place it near the door of your place of business to call in customers.

HIGH JOHN AND A SILVER DIME MOJO HAND
(from *"Cash Box Conjure"* by Miss Phœnix LeFæ)
Get a High John the Conqueror root that will fit in your pocket. Dress it with Money Drawing Oil and fold a soft and worn two dollar bill around it. Wind it and tie it with green thread and sew it into a tight-fitting chamois cover. Feed this hand with Money Drawing Oil at least once a week.

MACE IN PACKETS AND MOJO HANDS
The use of Mace arils to draw money makes sense because Mace grows attached to the Nutmeg, itself a celebrated money-drawing curio. However, unlike the hard, round Nutmeg, Mace is softly pliable and works well in flat packets when added to small seeds like Grains of Paradise and Fenugreek.

PUMPKIN PIE SPICE PROSPERITY PACKET
In powder form, Mace, Nutmeg, Allspice, Cloves, and Cinnamon — the so-called "pumpkin pie spices" — are all money herbs. Buy a pre-made spice blend, add a silver dime, and fold them, seed-packet style, into a 3" Post-It note on which you have written your wish. Carry this in your change purse.

FOR THE HEALTH OF YOUR BANK ACCOUNT
Rose hips — the fruits of the Rose bush — are good for health and general good fortune. They can also be dried and placed in a bag with a pyrite chunk and Mint for the health of your bank account.

PATCHOULI TO ATTRACT MONEY
Blend Patchouli leaves in equal parts with Sandalwood and Quassia chips and carry the mixture in a flannel bag dressed with Money Drawing Oil. This herb combination can also be laid down in the corners or sprinkled around the home or business.

A PYRITE AND LODESTONE MONEY MOJO
Place a small piece of Pyrite in a green flannel money-drawing mojo hand along with lodestones or money-luck herbs such as Cinnamon, Nutmeg, Allspice, Chamomile, Irish Moss, Bayberry, Alfalfa, and High John the Conqueror.

GUNPOWDER TO DRAW QUICK BUSINESS
Place a pinch of Gunpowder, two lodestone chips, and nine Red Pepper seeds on a piece of red flannel, fold toward you repeatedly to make a packet, and sew it up. Dress the packet with Money Drawing Oil and Crown of Success Oil and keep it in your cash register.

EARTH SMOKE TO MAKE QUICK SALES
The alternative names Fumitory and Earth Smoke both refer to this herb's popular use as a lucky incense, but it is just as commonly folded into a paper prayer or petition packet and worn in the shoe by salesmen, for luck in making quick sales.

FOR COMMISSION SALES OR TIPS
Get a Buckeye nut, a bunch of Allspice berries, and a special coin that you earned from a commission sale or received in a tip from a good customer. Wrap them in a piece of flannel with a small petition paper for money. You can use Psalms 23 and sign your full name to it if you have no words of your own. Carry this in your right pocket and sprinkle it every other day with Hoyt's Cologne to improve your success in business and ensure steady commissions or tips.

JOB-GETTING AND STEADY WORK MOJOS

A SILVER DIME HAND TO GET A JOB

Cut a small square of red flannel, put a silver dime in the center, and cover it with a pinch of graveyard dirt from someone who loved you. Fold the cloth toward you to draw your wish to you, fold it again, rotating the cloth each time so that you always fold toward you until you make a small, flat packet. Sew the packet shut and sprinkle it with Hoyt's Cologne. Wear it in your right shoe for nine days, dressing it every day with Hoyt's Cologne, then switch and wear it for nine more days in your left shoe, still dressing it every day. On the nineteenth day, apply for a job and you will get it.

A PAIR OF LUCKY ROCKS TO GET A JOB

In 1939 in Saint Petersburg, Florida, Informant #995 told Rev. Hyatt: "A man learnt me, a hoodoo man, to take a Crocus Fish — it's a little fish called Crocus Fish [Croaker Fish; Fresh-water Drumfish], and you take that head off, and you take a knife and split that head open and there's two rocks [otoliths] in there. Well, you get them two rocks out and you put them two rocks in a little bag and you sew that bag up. Well, when you sew that bag up, then you give it to the party [your client] and then he goes to the man and reports for a job, and he can't hardly be turned down. And I have seen that and he [the hoodoo man] have done me thataway, the reason I know, and that's the way he said, and that was the end of that."

A day later, while still in Saint Petersburg, Florida, Rev. Hyatt met another practitioner, Informant #1019, who shared a similar mojo: "I have tried this when I first came to Saint Petersburg. Go and look me round, couldn't get me a job nowhere. One fellow tells me, says, 'Now you go and take you a dime,' he say, 'and buy you a Crocus Fish [Fresh-water Drumfish].' After you get that fish, you cut the head off that fish and you can do what you wish — you can eat the fish or you can throw it away — but be sure you get the head of that fish and cut it open, and get them two rocks out of there and put them in a sack and wear it in your pocket. There can't nobody turn you down for a job."

GETTING A JOB, A PAY RAISE, AND A PROMOTION

Carry Gravel Root and salt when looking for a job or asking for a raise or a promotion. Add a pair of lucky rocks or a lucky coin, if you wish.

MOJOS TO KEEP THE MONEY YOU HAVE

THREE COINS TO TAKE OFF A MONEY-JINX

If your money-luck is jinxed, you may be able to bring cash in, but you won't be able to keep it. To take off that mess, carry reddish Alkanet, golden Chamomile, and one green uncrossing herb, such as Lemon Grass, Rue, or Agrimony. There should be three kinds of herbs, plus three kinds of coins — one copper, one golden-brass, and one silver — in the bag.

STEADY-MONEY MOJO HAND

To reduce expenses and keep a steady bank balance, combine Smart Weed, Fenugreek seeds, Irish Moss, Sarsaparilla, and Sassafras, plus one coin each of five different denominations, one coin for each herb. Carry these in a green bag anointed weekly with Special Oil Number 20.

BLUE FLAG AND PENNY FOR CONTINUED PROSPERITY

Carry Blue Flag root, Irish Moss, and an encased "Keep Me and Never Go Broke" penny in a green flannel bag, so your money will never run out.

BR'ER RABBIT'S MONEY MOJO

As described by Uncle Remus to Joel Chandler Harris, Br'er Rabbit himself kept a pinch of Collard seeds, a piece of Calamus root, and a Rabbit foot in a tasselled money-purse.

SASSAFRAS AND SCRIPTURES: CONTROL YOUR MONEY

If you want your money to go farther and last longer, sprinkle a pinch of Sassafras root on a copy of Deuteronomy 8:18 *("But thou shalt remember the Lord thy God: for it is he that giveth thee power to get wealth ...")* and put it in your wallet or purse, in contact with your cash.

LODESTONE AND SILVER COINS: ALWAYS HAVE MONEY

Miss Phœnix relates that Rev. Hyatt learned this spell in 1939 from Informant #1116, a female professional root doctor in Waycross, Georgia: "Lodestone is supposed to be a drawing power with your money. You place it with your money and you wear it around your waist with a dime or any silver piece of money. You put that lodestone around your waist and wear it, and it will bring you luck; you'll always have money."

TO MAKE YOUR MONEY GO FARTHER

Alfalfa seed has a similar use to the leaves: A small packet of it sewn shut and kept in your wallet is said to make your money last longer between pay days. Fenugreek seed is also used to draw in money, and the two types of seed (which are botanically related) may be combined in one packet, for added power.

STRONG MONEY-HOLDING MOJO HAND

Jam a silver dime into an Alligator foot so that it looks like the 'gator is grabbing the coin. Wrap it tightly with three windings around of red flannel cloth, sprinkling Sassafras root chips between each layer as you wind, and sew it tight. Just as the Alligator foot holds the coin and won't let go, so will you be able to save instead of spend.

PROTECT YOUR INVESTMENTS

If friends and relatives are always hitting on you for loans but are slow to repay, mix Sassafras, Cinnamon, Cloves, Irish Moss, and Alkanet in a green flannel bag. When a person asks to borrow from you, get two things from them — a hair from their head and their name on a little paper in their own handwriting. You don't need to explain why you want these things. Just say, *"I'll loan you the money if i can have a hair from your head and*  *your name written in your own handwriting on this little piece of paper."* If they want the money bad enough, they'll do as you say. Write your name across their name on the paper to control them. Around the crossed names, in a square, write, *"Faithful to a Trust"* four times, once on each side of the square, like four square walls boxing the names in. Fold the paper towards you, around the hair, folding toward you again and again until it is small. Place the paper packet in the bag, and they will repay the loan on time.

"SNAKE MASTER" MOJO TO PROTECT YOUR MONEY

Combine Black Snake Root, White Snake Root, Seneca Snake Root, Sampson Snake Root, Snake Weed, Rattlesnake Master, and Snake skin sheds to make a protective hand. Dress it with Protection Oil and keep it with your money. This will keep you from over-spending and it will also guard your money against theft, especially from known "Snakes in the grass."

MOJO HANDS TO GET A LOAN

AN ANCESTRAL MOJO FOR GETTING A LOAN

Get a small catalogue photo of what you want to purchase with the loan. On a small piece of paper write your monetary petition, signed with your name. On the other side of the petition write out Deuteronomy 8:18 *("But thou shalt remember the Lord thy God: for it is he that giveth thee power to get wealth, that he may establish his covenant which he sware unto thy fathers, as it is this day.")* Put a pinch each of Alfalfa, salt, and graveyard dirt on the papers and fold them seed packet style. The graveyard dirt should be from a male ancestor on your paternal line. If that is impossible, obtain the graveyard dirt of any ancestor. If no ancestral dirt is available, work with any paternal figure's grave. Buy the dirt with three coins while reciting Deuteronomy 8:18. Carry the packet in a green bag dressed with Crown of Success Oil when you go to the bank to ask for a loan. If possible, mention the Lord or your own father while talking with the loan officer.

FIVE FINGER GRASS TO GAIN A FAVOUR

According to John George Hohman, author of *"Pow Wows or The Long Lost Friend,"* if you call upon another to ask for a favour, carry a little of the Five Finger Grass with you, and you shall certainly obtain that which you desire. It is also carried when asking for a bank loan.

A MOJO FOR GETTING A LOAN TO BUY SOMETHING

Write your monetary petition *("Grant me the loan of $12,000.00")* or your affirmation *("The Bank of Umexa loans me $12,000.00")* or your prayer *("Dear Lord, Please sway the heart of Miss Sibley, the loan officer at the Bank of Umexa, that she may consent to loan me $12,000.00")* on a piece of paper and sign it with your name. On top of this, lay a small catalogue photo of whatever item you intend to purchase with the loan. On top of the photo place a pinch of Alfalfa leaves, a pinch of Five Finger Grass, and several whole Cloves. Wrap everything up into a packet and carry it in a green mojo bag dressed with Crown of Success Oil and Hoyt's Cologne when you go to the bank to ask for the loan.

For many more ways to draw money luck in gambling or business, see: **"Cash Box Conjure" by Miss Phœnix LeFæ**

Mojo bags, herbs, minerals, books, and oils offered in mail order hoodoo catalogues, 1925 - 2018. Art by Charles C. Dawson, Grey Townsend, and One Unknown Artist for Famous Products, King Novelty, Sovereign Products, and the Lucky Mojo Curio Co.

THE HAND OF POWER

CARRYING A MOJO FOR POWER

Personal power is measured in many ways: quick reflexes, bodily strength, muscle mass, tireless endurance, charismatic animal magnetism, respect, freedom from doubts or bad habits, heightened spiritual awareness, the gifts of divination and prophesy, or the ability to cast magic spells.

In this chapter you will find traditional mojo hands that are said to:

- **Enhance your ability to succeed in all mundane matters.**
- **Increase physical strength, energy, maturity, and power.**
- **Enhance wisdom, psychic gifts, and prophetic abilities.**
- **Encourage others to treat you with respect and decency.**
- **Help to overcome fear and anxiety; enhance courage and bravery.**
- **Keep away entangling legality; win court cases and lawsuits.**
- **Give you the power to brush aside or drive off enemies.**
- **Assist you in overcoming bad habits and addictions.**

MINERALS FOR POWER AND MASTERY

- **Epsom Salts:** For control over others; for physical health.
- **Goofer Dust:** To weaken or drive down your foes or enemies.
- **Graveyard Dirt:** For the assistance of the spirits present in the dirt.
- **Lodestone:** Will draw what you desire to you like a magnet.
- **Magnetic Sand:** To feed and energize the lodestones.
- **Salt and Rock Salt:** For purification, power, and protection.

INCENSE RESINS USED IN POWER MOJOS

- **Benzoin:** To take off jinxes that have affected the health.
- **Camphor Resin:** To drive off unwanted spirits.
- **Dragon's Blood Resin:** To draw favour, luck, and success.
- **Myrrh:** For the development of psychic powers and visions.
- **Pine Resin (Rosin):** For restoration after a negative spiritual attack.
- **Sandalwood:** To strengthen the spirit and remove negative conditions.

HERBS AND ROOTS FOR POWER AND HEALTH

These are the herbs, roots, and zoological curios used in hands of power:

- **Acacia Leaf:** For personal power, psychic visions, dealing with the dead.
- **Allspice Berries:** To relieve mental stress.
- **Althæa:** A healer; for psychic gifts and for healing from past sorrow.
- **Angelica Root:** It conveys the power and beauty of the angels.
- **Anise Seed:** For psychic visions and true dreams.
- **Asafœtida:** For protection from diseases and for the power to heal.
- **Ash Tree:** For healing and the maintenance of good health.
- **Bearberry:** For lucky and visionary divination.
- **Black Snake Root:** Strengthens those who are weak, timid, fearful, or shy.
- **Boldo:** To keep off diseases and also those who carry them.
- **Buckeye Nut:** To protect from headaches and rheumatism.
- **Calamus Root:** To bring another under your command.
- **Calendula Flowers:** For powerful lucky number dreams; to win in court.
- **Cascara Sagrada:** For protection from unjust legal charges.
- **Celery Seed:** Enhances psychic abilities and induce prophetic dreams.
- **Cinnamon:** For energy and activity in every type of undertaking.
- **Comfrey:** To improve health and safety, for regeneration after injuries.
- **Coriander Seeds:** For favour and success in court cases.
- **Cubeb Berries:** To compel your chosen mate to love you.
- **Dandelion Root:** To enhance psychic dreams for luck and power.
- **Deer's Tongue Leaf:** For eloquent speech in debates or court cases.
- **Devil's Shoe Strings:** To tie down bad spirits; to draw respect and favour.
- **Dill Seed:** To ward off natural and unnatural illnesses.
- **Fennel Seed:** To conduct your business in private.
- **Five Finger Grass:** For success in all the work that five fingers can do.
- **Flax Seed:** For psychic visions, and to cleanse away negative spirits.
- **Ginseng (Wonder of the World) Root:** For male strength and health.
- **Golden Seal Root:** For strength and healing from diseases and sorrows.
- **Grains of Paradise:** For the power to rise and achieve one's ambitions.
- **Hops:** For a restful night's sleep; to remove the fear of nightmares.
- **Huckleberry Leaves:** To dream true; for lucky prophetic dreams.
- **John the Conqueror Root:** For personal power, mastery, and strength.
- **Knot Weed:** To tie down your troubles, bad habits, and addictions.

- **Lavender:** For restful dreams without nightmares.
- **Lemon Verbena:** To clear space between people and drive them apart.
- **Licorice Root:** To gain power over others so that they follow you.
- **Little John to Chew Root:** For victory in legal and courtroom matters.
- **Master of the Woods:** For natural rulership over competitors.
- **Master Root:** For respect, authority, rulership, and mastery over others.
- **Mistletoe:** To remove jinxes and all psychic attacks on one's health.
- **Mojo Wishing Beans:** May all your dreams and wishes come true.
- **Motherwort:** For the power and strength of blessed motherhood.
- **Mugwort and Wormwood (Artemisia):** For psychic powers.
- **Mustard Seed, Black or Brown:** To keep enemies and snitches away.
- **Nettle:** To remove fear and to assist in overcoming difficulties.
- **Oregano:** For success against opponents in court and legal matters.
- **Peach Leaves:** For the power of concentration and memorization.
- **Peony Root:** For good health and long life.
- **Pepper, Black or Red:** To send away an enemy.
- **Poppy:** For psychic dreams and visions; to confuse enemies.
- **Primrose:** For children to show respect to their parents.
- **Queen Elizabeth Root:** For female power and strength.
- **Rattlesnake Rattle:** For courage in the face of danger.
- **Rose:** For blessings, graceful ease, and love.
- **Rosemary:** For the strength and rulership of women.
- **Rue:** To clear up any health problems caused by the evil eye.
- **Sage:** For memorization, understanding, and development of wisdom.
- **Sampson Snake Root:** To remove unnatural illness; to gain strength.
- **Self-Heal (All-Heal):** To heal oneself both physically and spiritually.
- **Shame Brier:** To cause those who accuse you in court to feel shame.
- **Solomon's Seal Root:** For the wisdom of King Solomon.
- **Southern John (Dixie John) Root:** For contentment within the family.
- **Star Anise:** For psychic visions and intuitive healing.
- **Sumac Berries:** For mercy of the court and a more lenient sentence.
- **Ten Bark:** To ward off and heal from fevers and unnatural illnesses.
- **Tobacco:** To contact people whose location is unknown; a spirit offering.
- **Vandal Root:** To send away competitors and enemies.
- **Verbena:** To take off jinxes that have affected your health.
- **Wahoo:** To take off crossed conditions and restore male virility.
- **Yarrow:** For psychic powers and courage in dangerous conditions.

DRESSING AND FEEDING A POWER MOJO

- **Abramelin Oil:** For spiritual and occult power and working with seals.
- **Aunt Sally's Lucky Dream Oil:** To remember lucky number dreams.
- **Black Arts Oil:** An aid in destructive spells and pact-making.
- **Block Buster Oil:** To blow apart blockages and obstacles in your way.
- **Cast Off Evil Oil:** To rid one of bad habits and wicked influences.
- **Commanding Oil:** For leadership skills when others follow you.
- **Compelling Oil:** To compel another to make good on a promise.
- **Controlling Oil:** For control over the actions and thoughts of others.
- **Court Case Oil:** To influence judge and jury to decide in your favour.
- **Crossing Oil:** To do unto enemies as they have done unto you.
- **Crown of Success Oil:** For financial, school, or career success.
- **Crucible of Courage Oil:** For determination, courage, and bravery.
- **Do As I Say Oil:** For the power to command others to obey.
- **Domination Oil:** To rule others and control them.
- **Essence of Bend-Over Oil:** For imposing one's will upon others.
- **Healing Oil:** For relief of sickness, sorrow, and physical problems.
- **Hot Foot Oil:** To drive unwanted persons from your life.
- **I Can You Can't Oil:** To hold another back so that you can get ahead.
- **Indian Spirit Guide Oil:** To call upon Blackhawk or other Native spirits.
- **Influence Oil:** To influence the thoughts or actions of others.
- **John the Conqueror Oil:** To increase personal power and mastery.
- **King Solomon Wisdom Oil:** For wisdom when making decisions.
- **Law Keep Away Oil:** For those who wish to conduct business in private.
- **Master Oil:** To aid one's ability to control situations and people.
- **Master Key Oil:** Used by those who seek occult and spiritual mastery.
- **Moses Oil:** A spiritual oil used to dress seals.
- **Nature Oil:** Said to increase the user's sexual vitality.
- **Power Oil:** To increase your personal strength and spiritual power.
- **Psychic Vision Oil:** To enhance spiritual insight and prophetic dreams.
- **Queen Elizabeth Root Oil:** For queenly female power.
- **Run Devil Run Oil:** To drive the Devil and his imps away.
- **Seven-Eleven Holy Oil:** For the blessings of the Lord on all ventures.
- **Spirit Guide Oil:** To encourage the aid of helpful, beneficent spirits.
- **Tobacco Oil:** Used in court case and spiritual contact work.
- **Whiskey:** Johnny Walker for health, Wild Turkey or Old Crow for spirit.

THE HAND OF STRENGTH

OLD INDIAN STRENGTH CHARM

High John the Conqueror root is not African; it entered hoodoo via Native American herb magic. The Iroquois call it Man-Root and believe it to be so powerful that children must not touch it. If a man carries a whole root on his persoj, they say, he will be strong enough to carry two Deer; if he touches his root before hitting someone, his strength will kill them.

"MASTER MOJO" FOR PHYSICAL STRENGTH

To gain in strength and power, and to perform well in sports, carry a red "Master Mojo" that contains Master Root, Master of the Woods, and Sampson Snake Root, dressed with John the Conqueror Oil. Women can use the same combination but dress the hand with Queen Elizabeth Root in Oil.

A LOUISIANA TOBY WITH LIGHTNING-STRUCK WOOD

In February 1940, while in New Orleans, Harry Hyatt met a person he called Informant #1524, who gave him the following toby:

"They tell you about the tree that's struck by lightning. You take the bark from that tree and you burn that bark into ashes and you take them ashes and you get you some Epsom salts and put it with that. You put it in a flannel rag with lodestone and you sew it up, and you take that and use it as a toby for all the time. If you want to go your way, just go on and go your way. Long as you got that with you, you can't never be disappointed, nobody will ever refuse you no way, and you'll never have no fusses."

This toby is almost identical to one that i purchased in 1965 in Oakland, California, from a man who had been born in Louisiana and called himself a "toby maker." The major difference was that he did not burn the wood from the lightning-struck tree to ashes. Rather, he used a pocket knife to split it into splinters. Everything else — the lodestone (fed with magnetic sand), the Epsom salts, and the red flannel rag — was the same.

A SOLOMONIC SEAL HAND FOR STRENGTH

Back in the 1970s i bought a mail-order "hand of strength" that was quite effective. It was made in red leather, filled with Cinnamon, Grains of Paradise, Rosemary, and Mojo Beans, and contained a folded First Pentacle of Mars for courage, ambition, enthusiasm and physical accomplishments.

THE HEALING HAND

TO WARD OFF DISEASE
Ash Tree leaves carried in a packet in combination with Asafœtida are thought to prevent disease and keep you healthy. Wear Asafœtida in a bag around the neck to ward off colds, flu, and contagious diseases.

TO HELP WARD OFF ILLNESS
Carry Dill seed, Flax seed, and an Angelica Root in a white flannel or muslin bag to keep away unnatural sickness. Dill seeds tied in a white handkerchief cloth and smelled are said to be a cure for hiccoughs.

TO TAKE OFF UNNATURAL ILLNESS
If you have been fed a magical poison, make a toby with Sampson Snake Root, Seneca Snake Root, and dried Pine sap. Soak Sampson Snake Root in Whiskey for a week. Drink a tablespoonful morning and night and use it to feed the mojo as well.

TEN BARK DISEASES
Ten Bark, an old-time medical plant, is worn in a bag at the neck to ward off diseases and unnatural illness. It is one of several Cinchona species from which the anti-malarial drug Quinine is derived. Add a pinch of Self Heal, a whole Angelica Root, and a pinch of Sandalwood and carry this hand in a red bag; it will keep the bearer in good health.

TO REGAIN LOST VIRILITY
To restore lost nature that has been taken by a woman who jinxed you (and not because of serious medical problems), make a strong tea of Sampson Snake Root and Wahoo root bark, and bathe the genitals in this every morning for three weeks. Carry a mojo made with these two roots, plus John the Conqueror Root, in your front pants pocket.

GOLDEN SEAL FOR BETTER HEALTH
Place Golden Seal root, Angelica Root, and Self Heal in a white bag or a handkerchief. Add a charm or holy medal to help in health matters. Dress the bag with Holy Oil or Blessing Oil, and sew it into the mattress of a loved one who suffers chronic pain, serious disease, or acute illness.

PROTECTION FROM ILLNESS AND SNAKE BITE

To ward off jinxing illness, carry Boneset leaves in a mojo bag with Angelica Root and Devil's Shoe Strings. Boneset's alternative name White Snake Root indicates that the plant also protects from Snake bite.

TO HELP OR HEAL SOMEONE DEAR TO YOU

A single Peony root carried in a mojo bag, with a small cross and the hair of the person for whom the work is being done wrapped in their name paper, is believed to ward off evil of any kind, natural or unnatural, to break jinxes, and even to cure mental illness or substance abuse that was brought onto the person by a curse. The bag is dressed with Protection Oil, Blessing Oil, Cast Off Evil Oil, or Run Devil Run Oil, according to the circumstances.

FOR PROTECTION FROM RHEUMATISM

Carry a Buckeye nut in the front pocket and oil it on your nose to shine it up. This will keep off rheumatism. To make a hand with it, add Snake skin sheds (Snakes are supple) and Willow leaves or bark (Willow is flexible).

TO CLEAR UP HEALTH MATTERS

Rue carried with Comfrey root is said to improve health and to promote regeneration after injuries. Rue, Comfrey root, Verbena, Mistletoe, and Benzoin carried in a bag will take off jinxes affecting the health.

TO ENABLE A CHILD TO TEETHE WITHOUT PAIN

Take a raw egg, write the baby's name on it in ink, place it in a muslin Tobacco sack, and hang it over the door to the baby's bedroom. The egg will dry out, and the child will teethe without pain.

TO BLESS A NEW BABY

Place a whole Angelica Root, an Althæa root or leaves, a pinch of Flax seed, and some Rose buds in a white flannel mojo bag. Dress the bag with Blessing Oil and keep it near where the baby sleeps.

HEALTH-PROTECTING PINE RESIN MOJO

Pine tree resin (also called rosin) drives out spirits, including those that cause disease. If mixed with crumbled Camphor and Boldo leaves and carried in red flannel, the result is a strong health-protecting hand.

POWER TO OVERCOME DIFFICULTIES

YARROW AND NETTLE FOR COURAGE AND BRAVERY
Write your fears on a piece of paper, cross them with your name written nine times, carry the name paper in a yellow bag with a pinch each of Yarrow and Nettle, and you will overcome your fears.

RATTLESNAKE RATTLE FOR COURAGE AND POWER
Carry a Rattlesnake rattle as an emblem of courage, mastery, and luck. To keep it from fragmenting, place it in a small bottle or metal case. Sadly, Rattlesnakes are becoming endangered over much of their native territory, so i advise only buying a vintage rattle collected in decades past.

A MOJO FOR MASTERY OVER ADVERSE CONDITIONS
Master of the Woods, Master Root, and Grains of Paradise bring courage and luck when under stress while dealing with authority figures.

KNOT WEED TO REMOVE PROBLEMS AND BAD HABITS
Use something small to symbolize your problem — a bit of the drug or Tobacco that is hurting you, a folded-up paper upon which you have written a description of the problem, or a photograph of whatever is tempting you. Mix Knot Weed with soft beeswax and form it into a ball around the object, as you speak aloud your desire for your problems to be gone. Instead of carrying this ball, bury it in a graveyard and ask the spirits of the dead to keep your problem until you return; then walk away.

ANGELICA TO RELIEVE ANXIETY, SUSTO, OR FEAR
Mexicans say that if a girl or young woman has been badly frightened, she should carry a whole Angelica Root in a white bag. If she was frightened by a man, add a holy card of the Archangel Michæl.

ALLSPICE ROOTS BAG TO RELIEVE MENTAL TENSION
Some folks carry a cloth packet of Allspice berries on their person to ease their minds when they are under stress. To make this into a root bag, combine the Allspice berries with any two of the following roots, for a total of three ingredients: John the Conqueror Root, Master Root, Sampson Snake Root, Solomon's Seal Root, or Ginseng Root.

POWER OVER OTHERS

JOHN THE CONQUEROR MOJO FOR PERSONAL POWER
To conquer obstacles, carry a whole John the Conqueror Root dressed daily with Crown of Success Oil. When making a mojo bag for this purpose, a popular threesome of ingredients is John the Conqueror Root, Master Root, and Sampson Snake Root in a red flannel bag.

THREE ROOTS FOR PERSONAL POWER AND SUCCESS
Carry Peony root, Calamus root, and Solomon Seal Root in a red flannel bag. Dress the bag with John the Conqueror Oil for power, Crown of Success Oil for success, or Crown Royal Whiskey for both conditions.

LICORICE AND CALAMUS TO GAIN COMPLIANCE
Write the names of those you wish to rule on a piece of paper nine times. Add Licorice root and Calamus root for control, a tiny lodestone fed with magnetic sand, and a pinch each of table salt, Epsom salts, and rock salt. Add their hairs if you can get them. Fold the paper and carry it in a red bag dressed with Essence of Bend-Over, Influence, and Domination Oils.

TO GAIN THE RESPECT OF OTHERS ON THE JOB
A powerful mojo hand for obtaining and keeping increased respect on the job can be made by combining Sampson Snake Root, Master Root, and Gravel Root in a purple bag, such as a Crown Royal Whiskey mini-bottle bag, and dressing it with Crown of Success Oil and Crown Royal Whiskey.

DRAGON'S BLOOD MOJO TO GAIN RESPECT AND FAVOUR
Dragon's Blood resin, Solomon's Seal Root, John the Conqueror chips, Devil's Shoe Strings, and Five-Finger Grass carried in a red flannel bag will draw respect, favour, success, and friendship to you.

PRIMROSE MOJO FOR RESPECTFUL CHILDREN
An old-fashioned garden flower, Primrose brings peace to the home by causing children to respect and mind their parents. Hide the dried leaves and flowers in a muslin bag in your children's pillows with Hops flowers and Motherwort. After a week, the mojos will be attuned to the children, so you may steep the bags in hot water to make a tea and add this to their baths.

HANDS THAT HARM AND HURT

A RED PEPPER PACKET SPELL TO UNDERMINE AN ENEMY
To slowly weaken an enemy or competitor, fold Red Pepper, whole Black Pepper, and graveyard dirt into a paper on which you have written the enemy's name. Fold the paper packet into a black cloth, tie it with black thread, and hide it in the enemy's house, car, or place of business.

VANDAL ROOT PACKET TO JINX AN ENEMY'S CAR
Put your enemy's name or photo face-down under a black candle dressed with Black Arts Oil. Surround it with a ring of Vandal Root. When the candle is finished, tie the Vandal Root and his name paper or photo in a handkerchief and hide it in his car, so that he will wreck or have bad luck with the car.

TO STOP AN ENEMY'S LUCK AND SEND HIM AWAY
Place Knot Weed, Devil's Shoe String Root, and the enemy's picture or name paper on a black cloth. Dress it with Crossing Powder, and tie it into a bundle with black thread. Every day for three days, step on it and say, *"[Name], may your luck go away"* three times. On the fourth day, throw it into a river and say, *"As this bundle goes away, so will [Name] go away."*

A BREAK-UP PACKET UNDER A COUPLE'S DOORSTEP
To bring strife and divorce to a couple, steal a piece of clothing or a photo from each, place Lemon Verbena between the two items, wrap it all up in cloth, and bury the packet under the doorstep where they must cross over it.

AUNT MYMEE'S TRICKER BAG FOR DISGRACE OR DEATH
In 1893, Mary Alicia Owen described a tricker bag made by Aunt Mymee, a former slave of African and Native descent: "Take the wing of a jaybird, the jaw of a squirrel, and the fang of a rattle-snake and burn them to ashes on any red-hot metal. Mix the ashes with a pinch of grave-dust […], moisten with the blood of a pig-eating sow; make into a cake and stick into the cake three feathers of a crowing hen wrapped with hair from the head of the one who wishes an enemy tricked. Put the cake into a little bag of new linen or cat-skin. […] tied with a ravelling from a shroud, named for the enemy, and then hidden under his house. It will bring upon him disease, disgrace, and sorrow. If a whippoorwill's wing is used instead of a jay's it will bring death."

COURT CASE MOJOS

FENNEL AND OREGANO TO KEEP THE LAW AWAY
Mix Fennel seed, Oregano, and Black Mustard Seed and carry them in a blue flannel bag with three chips of Cascara Sagrada bark, dressed with Law Keep Away Oil, when you wish to conduct business in private. Asafœtida is a bit strong smelling, but it too is said to keep off the police and thus it may be added to this hand.

TOBACCO AND DEER'S TONGUE FOR SPEECH IN COURT
Carry Tobacco mixed with salt and Deer's Tongue in a knotted handkerchief in your pocket for success in court. Deer's Tongue makes for good speech, so it can help your lawyer, or help you, if you will testify.

A SEVEN-HERB COURT CASE MOJO
Write the names of those who oppose you on a piece of brown grocery-bag paper and cross them with your name written three times. Wrap a pinch each of Calendula, Anise seed, Deer's Tongue, Celery seed, Tobacco snuff, Cascara Sagrada, and Dill seed in the paper, folding away from you and saying, *"May this trouble be removed from me."* Tie the packet with thread and carry it in your pocket when you go to court. In the courtroom, chew a Little John to Chew Root and spit it onto the paper mojo hand to feed it.

NAME PAPERS AND LITTLE JOHN COURT CASE MOJO
If you oppose others in court, whether as plaintiff or defendant, write all of your opponents' names on paper, cross them with your name written nine times, wrap the name paper around a Little John Root and dress it with Court Case Oil. Place this packet in a bag with Calendula, Cascara Sagrada, Dill seed, Deer's Tongue, and Oregano.

CASCARA SAGRADA AND LITTLE JOHN FOR COURT
Light a brown candle dressed with Court Case Oil, burn Cascara Sagrada on charcoal, and pray the 35th Psalm for deliverance every day for nine days before your court date. Carry Cascara Sagrada, Calendula, and Tobacco snuff into court in a mojo bag, and chew a prepared Little John Root so that the judge will favour your case.

TO CONFUSE COURT PROCEEDINGS

Black Mustard seeds keep the police away by confusing them, but if you are arrested, carry the seeds in your pocket with Poppy seeds when going to court, so disruptive confusion will arise among the prosecution lawyers and the witnesses against you, and you will go free or receive a light sentence.

DILL AND CORIANDER FOR COURT CASES

Write the names of all the parties on paper in red ink, wrap the paper in red cloth, and sprinkle it with Dill seeds and Coriander seeds. Keep this charm in a cold, dark place — even going so far as to freeze it in a block of water — for nine days before the court date, or until you have won.

TO GET A LAWSUIT AGAINST YOU DROPPED

Cut pieces of Broom Straw, four inches long, out of a broom, one straw for each party to the court action who may harm you, including all witnesses, attorneys, and the judge. Brooms are used to sweep away people, and this spell will remove them from your life. Find a growing Shame Brier, pass your hands over its leaves, and as they faint, call each party's name and say, *"[Name], be shamed."* Dig a piece of the Shame Brier root four inches long and bundle the Straws around it with thread, making one turn around and tying one knot for each party. As you make each wrap and tie each knot, call out again *"[Name], be shamed."* Next, dig a piece of Rattlesnake Master root that is longer than the other pieces, say five inches long. As you dig it, call your own name and say, *"I, [Name], am the Master."* This root represents you and is longer and stronger than the others. Wrap and tie the Rattlesnake Master root to the bundle of driven-away and shamed parties, making one wrap and tying one knot for each person, calling out each one by name again as you tie the knot, saying, *"[Name], thus do i master you."* Roll the bundle in red flannel and sew it up very tight, then place it in a red flannel bag. Carry the bag in your pocket, and the lawsuit will either be dropped outright or, if it comes to court, it will be settled in your favour.

A LAST-DITCH LAW TRICK

If you have been found guilty in a court case, it is said that you can still help yourself if you gather nine berries from a Sumac plant and carry them in a bag in your pocket when you go before the judge for sentencing, for you will receive a lighter sentence or a smaller fine.

THE HAND OF PROTECTION

CARRYING A MOJO FOR SAFETY

Quite a few of us find ourselves at times having to deal with unpleasant people, work at dangerous jobs, or travel far from home among strangers. Ensuring our safety and walking shielded from negative energies, magical, attacks, and the assaults of ill-intentioned bullies, criminals, and enemies is vital. If you expect to be exposed to harm, a protective hand can help you.

In this chapter you will find mojo hands that will:

- **Protect from physical or magical attack by enemies.**
- **Protect from physical or magical attack by family, friends, or lovers.**
- **Shield your from unnatural illness.**
- **Ward off the evil eye of jealousy.**
- **Protect against back-biting and gossip.**
- **Protect and shield against racial profiling.**
- **Repel witchcraft and hag-riding at night.**
- **Protect your home from natural and unnatural disasters.**
- **Prevent theft or robbery in your home or your vehicle.**
- **Prevent accidents at work or on the job.**
- **Forestall accidents or breakdowns on the road.**

MINERALS FOR PROTECTION

Here is a list of minerals included in the protective mojos in this chapter:

- **Alum:** To stop the mouths of those who would slander you.
- **Blueing:** To uncross crossed conditions, to heal damage.
- **Graveyard Dirt:** To enlist the aid of helpful spirits.
- **Lodestone and Magnetic Sand:** For concentrated power.
- **Nails:** To nail down or harm those who do evil.
- **Needles and Pins:** To pierce or prick those who are evil.
- **Salt:** For protection from evil; for uncrossing, and breaking jinxes.
- **Silver Dime:** To protect against tricks laid in your path.
- **Sulphur:** To drive off evil with the fumes of the Devil.

HERBS AND ROOTS FOR PROTECTION

There are many herbs, roots, and zoological curios that can be included in mojo hands for protection and safety. You will not need all of these, of course — and if you must, you can substitute one for another of similar use.

- **Agrimony:** To send back curses that have already been cast.
- **Alder:** For protection against enemies.
- **Alkanet:** Stops those who try to trouble your money or jinx your luck.
- **Althæa:** To attract helper spirits, heal and soothe, and find treasure.
- **Angelica:** For power and strength; to protect women and children.
- **Anise Seed:** To ward off the evil eye; for psychic discernment.
- **Ash Tree:** For protection of friends and family members.
- **Aspand:** To destroy the evil eye and bring peace and happiness.
- **Balm of Gilead Buds:** To protect lovers or married people from envy.
- **Basil:** To remove evil from the home and to ward off the evil eye.
- **Bay Leaves:** For general protection and to avoid being jinxed.
- **Black Snake Root:** To strengthen weak, timid, fearful, or shy people.
- **Burdock Root:** To keep off jinxes; for personal protection.
- **Calamus:** For controlling rulership; it protects by dominating foes.
- **Caraway Seed:** For protection and to keep young children safe.
- **Cardamom:** To keep a marriage or love affair secure from enemies.
- **Cat's Eye Shell:** To ward off the evil eye and to break jinxes.
- **Celandine:** To keep off witches and law officers; it confuses foes.
- **Chamomile Flowers:** For taking off crossed conditions.
- **Clover Flowers, White:** To protect from evil influences.
- **Cloves:** To stop slander, malicious gossip, and damaging lies.
- **Comfrey Root:** For safety and health while travelling away from home.
- **Cumin Seeds:** To keep away evil from home.
- **Devil Pod or Bat Nut:** Strong protection from evil.
- **Devil's Bit:** To keep off jinxes and bad spirits.
- **Devil's Dung:** To end crossing or take off a jinx by counter-attack.
- **Devil's Shoe Strings:** Tangles up the Devil to protect you from evil.
- **Dill Seed:** To ward off illness and to protect sexuality and love.
- **Elder:** For protection from criminals and also from the law.
- **Elecampane:** For protection against witches.
- **Fenugreek seeds:** To protect your money and to get more money.

- **Fern:** To prevent jinxes, remove evil spirits, and ward off burglars.
- **Feverfew:** To prevent accidents in the home or while on the road.
- **Five Finger Grass:** To ward off evil and bring good luck.
- **Flax seeds:** For the protection and the health of children.
- **Gall of the Earth:** To protect money and treasures of all kinds.
- **Golden Seal:** To ward off evil and bring good luck in health matters.
- **Grains of Paradise:** For good luck and for protection of the home.
- **Hyssop:** To put an end to crossed conditions; to take off a jinx.
- **John the Conqueror:** For personal power, strength, and protection.
- **Little John to Chew:** For protection in court and from slander.
- **Mint:** To break spells and jinxes; to provide safety for self or home.
- **Motherwort:** For the protection of women and children.
- **Mugwort:** For eliminating interference in one's travel plans.
- **Mullein:** To drive away spiritual enemies and dangerous wild animals.
- **Mustard Seed, White:** For protection, safety, and blessings.
- **Nettle:** To break or take off curses and jinxes.
- **Onion:** For healing and for peace and luck in the home.
- **Oregano:** To keep troublesome people away.
- **Patchouli:** To break jinxes and curses.
- **Peony:** To protect against misfortune, break jinxes, and prolong life.
- **Pepper, Black:** To get rid of evil and to protect a person or place.
- **Pepper, Red, Cayenne:** To drive off enemies and get rid of evil.
- **Plantain:** To protect one against Snakes and also against thieves.
- **Quince Seeds:** To ward off the evil eye and to provide safety.
- **Rattlesnake Master:** To ward off actual and symbolic "Snakes."
- **Rose:** To remove a love-jinx by strengthening love.
- **Rosemary:** To protect against evil; especially good for women.
- **Rue:** To break hexes or jinxes; to repel the evil eye.
- **Sandalwood:** To protect the home and person; for blessings.
- **Sassafras:** To control your money and remove any ill-luck put on it.
- **Slippery Elm:** To stop gossip and slander by sliding it off of you.
- **Star Anise:** To stop misfortunes; to repel the evil eye.
- **Sugar:** To sweeten those who might otherwise try to harm you.
- **Verbena:** For protection against witches.
- **Wood Betony:** Protective against evil spirits and disease.
- **Wormwood:** For protection; prevents accidents.
- **Yarrow:** To break curses, aid psychic power, and stimulate courage.

DRESSING AND FEEDING A PROTECTION MOJO

- **Archangel Michæl Oil:** To guard Heaven from the onslaughts of Satan, and people from evil; the so-called "Policeman's Saint."
- **Cast Off Evil:** To drive off bad or dangerous companions; to remove the temptation to enter into unwanted behaviours or habits.
- **Fear Not To Walk Over Evil Oil:** To protect from tricks that may have been laid in your pathway or where you may walk over them.
- **Fiery Wall of Protection Oil:** To ward off and blast those who dare to attack or cause harm in any way.
- **Guardian Angel Oil:** To call upon your own angelic guardian spirit for aid in times of danger.
- **Hoyt's Cologne:** Add some salt and blueing to it, shake it up as you pray, and use it for safety.
- **Jinx Killer Oil:** To destroy jinxes and bad luck tricks that have been put on you.
- **King Solomon Wisdom Oil, Solomon's Seal Root in Oil:** To dress the edges of Solomonic seals of protection.
- **Protection Oil:** To call upon a protective spirit for aid in times of trouble or fear.
- **Reversing Oil:** To send back evil thoughts, words, or deeds to those who have sent or intend to send them to you.
- **Rue in Oil:** To do away with the evil eye of jealousy and for general protection from harm.
- **Run Devil Run Oil:** To cause negative people and entities to flee at your approach and bother you no more.
- **Safe Travel Oil:** To avoid accidents, unfair traffic stops, or breakdowns while on the road or in strange places.
- **Stop Gossip Oil:** To keep your name out of the mouths of backbiters, rivals, competitors, or nosy people.
- **Uncrossing Oil:** To remove crossed conditions or break a jinx and to keep the problem from returning.
- **Van Van Oil:** To clear away and keep away evil and to change bad luck to good luck.
- **Whiskey:** Johnny Walker for Safe Travel; Old Grand-Dad or Ancient Age for ancestral protection.

UNCROSSING AND JINX-BREAKING HANDS

JINX-BREAKING MOJO
Carry Burdock root, Rue, Agrimony, Black Snake Root, and a silver coin in a muslin bag or tied in a white handkerchief to keep off jinxes.

WARD OFF EVIL BY REVERSING IT TO THE SENDER
Some people like to carry a Devil Pod in a red flannel bag and anoint it with Uncrossing or Cast Off Evil Oil when they are surrounded by enemies. They work best in a purse or glove box as they are sharp!

UNCROSS YOURSELF OR BREAK A CURSE
For protection from crossed conditions, carry Mint in your shoe; for strength to break and conquer a curse, keep Mint in a mojo bag with a whole Calamus root and a whole High John the Conqueror Root.

VERBENA TO BREAK A JINX THAT CAUSED A FEVER
A packet of Verbena worn on the body is said to help those suffering from fever or poisoning as the result of a curse. The mojo can be fixed by smoking it in the fumes of Verbena, Sandalwood, and Agrimony burned on charcoal. Afterward, dress it with Uncrossing Oil.

AGRIMONY TO BREAK A JINX OR TURN BACK A SPELL
Mix Agrimony and Patchouli with graveyard dirt, and carry the mixture in a mojo bag to turn back a curse or a jinx.

THREE NAILS MAKE A JOMO AGAINST HAG-RIDING
Hoodoo is African-American folk magic, but this one comes second-hand. On August 19, 1939, a White man named Albert Spaulding, age 21, born in 1918, was the assistant manager of the commissary at Aycock & Lindsey turpentine camp in Cross City, Florida. The interview, conducted by Stetson Kennedy and recorded by Robert Cook, is included in the Florida Folklife section of the WPA Collections at the Library of Congress. Spaulding told of a black man he knew who bought three nails and a paper bag to make a protective "Joe Mow" to keep under his pillow as a preventive against attacks by hag-riding witches who would trouble him in his sleep. Very likely Psalms 91 was to be written on the paper bag.

HANDS THAT PROTECT AGAINT ENVY

TO PROTECT AGAINST THE EVIL EYE OF JEALOUSY
A matched pair of Balm of Gilead Buds is widely believed to protect lovers or a married couple against curses, hexes, and jinxes, and to ward off the evil eye of jealousy. Add them to any protection bag or mojo that is used for gambling, so that envious people cannot jinx your luck.

PROTECTION AGAINST THE EVIL EYE
Carry Rue, Aspand, and Cloves in a cloth bag or place it above the door to ward off the evil eye.

STAR ANISE TO WARD OFF ENVY
Many folks like to carry a whole Star Anise pod in a conjure bag to ward off the evil eye or *mal occhio*. If an entire pod is too large for your bag, collect the shiny seeds from nine Star Anise pods and use them instead.

ANISE AS AN APOTROPAIC CHARM
A pinch of Anise seed knotted up in your handkerchief and carried in the pocket is a simple protective measure against the evil eye. Its strength is said to be increased if it is combined with at least two other protective curios, such as Rue, Cat's Eye Shell, or Agrimony, thus fixing it up as a mojo hand.

STOP GOSSIP WITH ALUM AND NAMES IN A BAG
It was a cold, rainy day in March, 1939, when Rev. Hyatt set up his recorder at the Cooper Hotel in Waycross, Georgia, and met Informant #1152, who shared this mojo: "Take alum, a piece about big as a dime, and pound it up and put it in a little sack, and write the name of the party that you think that's interfering and put the name in the sack with that and wear it in your pocket. That would eliminate that trouble. They couldn't hurt you." Just as alum puckers up the mouth, so will this charm bag keep the person named from gossiping about you or messing in your business.

PROTECTION FROM ENVY AND SLANDER
Carry Cat's Eye shell in a red flannel bag with Rue and Slippery Elm for immunity from harmful tales told by covetous neighbours, back-biters on the job, and hidden enemies posing as friends.

HANDS TO PROTECT YOURSELF

ALDER ROOT FOR PROTECTION FROM ENEMIES
This job begins in the swamp, moves to the graveyard and ends with a mojo. It takes time and effort, but it is extremely powerful.

If you have enemies from whom you need strong protection, go to a stream or swamp where Alders grow and dig up a live piece of Alder root. Chop it fine, mix it with a half-handful of salt, and leave it to sit.

Next, take three silver dimes, three wooden matches, and three new sewing pins to a graveyard. Stick the pins upright into the match heads, stab the matches upright into the ground in a triangle formation, until the pin heads are flush with the ground, and then lay a silver dime atop each pin head. Scrape up a half-handful of graveyard dirt from within the triangle, leaving the dimes in place to pay the spirits of the dead for their dirt. As you lift up the dirt, say aloud, *"The Lord giveth and the Lord taketh away. Blessed be the Lord."*

Walk straight out of the graveyard backwards with the dirt in your hand, and then turn and walk home. When you get there, add the graveyard dirt to the chopped-up Alder root and salt. Cover the mixture with a quart of water and boil it until all the water has evaporated, but do not let it burn.

When all is dried and cooled, add a teaspoonful of gunpowder to it. Sew the combination into a piece of red flannel and wear it around your waist or at your neck, and it is said that nothing your enemies do can hurt you.

RATTLESNAKE MASTER AND A DIME IN A TOBY
In 1938, Rev. Hyatt learned this from Informant #650 in Mobile, Alabama: "You get a small piece of Rattlesnake Master and a small piece of High John the Conker Root and a new dime and a piece of lodestone, and you sew this into a little bag called a toby. Sew it up and you can either put it in a piece of red flannel or chamois skin. Sew that up in it and keep it into your left pocket always and never let anyone touch it. If you do that, that is a wonderful thing. That will prevent anyone from harming you."

FOR PROTECTION FROM AN UNRULY MAN
Women who are troubled because of a former relationship with a hurtful, unruly, or violent man carry a whole Angelica Root in a conjure bag dressed with Fiery Wall of Protection Oil.

LODESTONE AND BROKEN NEEDLE FOR PROTECTION

In February 1938, Rev. Hyatt picked up an unusual protection mojo in Mobile, Alabama, from a worker who was only known as Informant #674: "I hear that you can get a piece of lodestone and take a needle and break it in three parts and on a Friday morning — be sure it's on a Friday morning — and lay each part of that needle along the side of that lodestone. Sew it up in a red piece of flannel and wear it and they can't do you no harm."

THIRTEEN KINDS OF SEEDS FOR PROTECTION

Seeds are little packets of life encased in protective shells, and this mojo uses lucky seeds for protection. You will want from three to thirteen types, but just a pinch of each: Peony seeds to protect life, White Mustard seeds against curses, Star Anise seeds to stop misfortune and ward off the evil eye, Dill Seeds to protect love, Flax seeds to preserve health, Cumin seeds to safeguard the home, Caraway seeds for protection and healing, Anise seeds to repel the evil eye, Fenugreek seeds to protect money, Cardamom seeds to safeguard love, Grains of Paradise seeds for spiritual security, Red Pepper seeds to keep off evil, and Black pepper seeds to keep off jinxes. Mix them together, tie them in a square of cloth, and feed the hand with whiskey.

MOJO FOR SAFETY AT WORK

To prevent accidents on the job, especially if doing outdoor construction, stonework, landscaping, or roofing, carry Feverfew, Hyssop, and Rosemary in a mojo hand, with a small copy of Psalms 91: 11-12 (*"For he shall give his angels charge over thee, to keep thee in all thy ways. They shall bear thee up in their hands, lest thou dash thy foot against a stone."*)

BAY LEAF IN A BAG TO STOP INTERFERENCE

Carry Bay leaf in a mojo to stop interference by unwanted people. If the interference is legal, add Oregano and Little John to Chew. If it is social, add Black Snake Root and Blue Cohosh. If it is spiritual, add Mullein and Nettle.

NINE HERB PROTECTION AGAINST WITCHCRAFT

A nine-herb blend of Verbena, Yarrow, Wood Betony, Elecampane, Rue, Mugwort, Celandine, Nettle, and White Clover is an old European-style protective tea used as a protective bath against witches — but if you don't make them up into tea, you can carry them in a bag as a mojo.

DEVIL'S SHOE STRINGS MOJO FOR PROTECTION

Nine Devil's Shoe Strings are particularly powerful for protection from crossed conditions when carried in a red flannel bag. In making such a combination, use either three or seven ingredients — the others might be a silver dime, Peony root, Elder bark, a blueing ball, High John the Conqueror Root, Rue, or any well-known protection herbs. Feed the hand with Protection Oil or Whiskey to keep it working.

A "DEVIL HAND" FOR PROTECTION

Combine a whole Devil's Bit root, nine pieces of Devil's Shoe Strings root, and a Devil Pod in a black leather bag. On a small piece of paper, write the name of the person from whom you want to protect yourself, cross and cover the name with your name written three times, and fold the name paper around a pinch of Devil's Dung, folding away from you each time until it is a small packet. Dress the packet with Run Devil Run Oil and place it in the bag. This is among the strongest reversing hands that can be made, but you may have to find and dig your own Devil's Bit, or grow it in your garden, for the whole root is not always available in commerce.

DEVIL'S BIT PROTECTIVE MOJO

Devil's Bit root chips can be added to any protection mojo bag. It works well in conjunction with herbs like Rue, Aspand, and Agrimony.

RATTLESNAKE MASTER PROTECTION BAG

In March 1939, Rev. Hyatt interviewed rootworkers in a black-owned hotel in Brunswick, Georgia. That's where a person known as Informant #1207a shared a double recipe for making Rattlesnake Master Cologne and a matching mojo: "It's a commonest thing, a piece of root you call Rattlesnake Master. Well, you can get hold of a piece of Rattlesnake Master and you could cut it up, a piece of it, and put it into a bottle, see. You pour a bottle of cologne on it, see, and you stop it up and you set it to one side in your corner. After nine days you can take that stuff, you take it if you're going out 'round anywheres. You just — every time you go out, well, you just pour some of that in your hand and you take it and rub it all over your face. And then you take another piece of Rattlesnake Master and sew it into a bag. Take string then, and let it tie 'round your waist and wear that, see. And that keeps down all evil. That's protection — that's your protection."

SALT, SULPHUR, AND GRAVEYARD DIRT PROTECTION

In April 1939, in the home of Henry L. Timmons, in Florence, South Carolina, Rev. Hyatt interviewed a rootworker known as Informant #1295, who described this protective mojo: "Now this salt and brimstone and graveyard dirt is used for many things. See, that salt and brimstone, table salt and sulphur, you can take and burn it together, see, [to protect a home]. Then you can make a sack of those three things: salt and brimstone and graveyard dirt. See, that is called a bodyguard, body protection — make a sack of that. And every nine days saturate that good and well with camphorated oil. That will keep — not sin — but it will keep the evil spirits off you, using a little graveyard dust in that. They can't harm you."

BLACK SNAKE ROOT FOR PROTECTION

Add Black Snake Root chips to a protective mojo, or get a whole root, a silver dime, and rock salt, tie it with nine knots, and wear it at your waist.

SALT, SALTPETER, AND LODESTONE AGAINST ENEMIES

In July 1937, Rev. Hyatt interviewed rootworkers at a black-owned hotel in Jacksonville, Florida. That's where Informant #592 shared this mojo: "You get you a little bit of saltpeter and a little table salt and a little, tiny lodestone and you put that together. Get you a piece of red flannel, just a red, little, chamois-cloth, like. Roll those up in the red flannel and make a knot in it. You take you a string and tie it up and wear it around your waist. And you feed that thing with Hoyt's Cologne for nine days, and that breaks it up. They can't come there. If they trying to do something to you, that will keep it away."

RED PEPPER, SUGAR, AND LODESTONE MOJO

In Memphis, Tennessee, in May 1938, a man known as Informant #936 told Rev, Hyatt: "Get lodestone, Cayenne Pepper, and sugar — not salt, sugar. Get genuine lodestone from the drugstore and you get you some sugar and Cayenne Pepper, not Black Pepper, and sew it into a flannel and wear it right in your hip pocket where your watch go in at. And that opposes your enemies. They can't harm you."

ANGELICA AND MUSTARD SEEDS FOR PROTECTION

Carry White Mustard seeds and a whole Angelica Root in a white flannel bag and anoint it with 7-11 Holy Type Oil for spiritual protection.

HANDS TO PROTECT YOUR FAMILY

A MOJO TO PROTECT A BABY
Place Flax seeds in a white flannel bag with a whole Angelica Root anointed with Blessing Oil, add in a small picture of the Guardian Angel, and keep the bag near the baby.

A TOBY FOR THE BABY
Some folks place Caraway seeds, Angelica Root, Golden Seal root, Flax seeds, and Motherwort in a bag, anoint this conjure hand with 7-11 Holy Oil or Blessing Oil, and hang it over the baby's crib or tuck it into the stroller to ward off illness and harm.

A SEED PACKET TO PROTECT THE BABY
If you fear that the envious gaze of strangers may harm your baby, sew a cloth packet of Caraway, Dill, and Aspand seeds into his or her clothes.

TO PROTECT CHILDREN FROM HARM
When your children lose their baby teeth, keep them in a packet or container filled with Flax seed, to which you have added a shiny dime from the year of each child's birth, with the child's initials scratched into the coin. It doesn't matter if you don't get all the teeth — even one is a powerful personal concern and will be sufficient.

BLESSING AND PROTECTION
You can keep a packet of Motherwort with your family photos for blessing and protection, or make a three-way hand with Motherwort, Althæa, and Flax Seeds in a folded seed-packet paper on which you have written the names of all the family members.

TO PROTECT FAMILY AND FRIENDS
If you are worried about the safety of friends or family, put his or her photo or name paper in a yellow flannel or chamois conjure bag with Ash Tree leaves, an Angelica root, and a Comfrey root and mail it to the person to carry. To work without contact, keep the same sort of bag near the person's photograph. You may place it under an overturned bowl or saucer and burn a candle atop it to reach out to them.

HANDS TO PROTECT YOUR HOME

ANGELICA TO STOP EVIL FROM ENTERING YOUR HOME
Place a whole Angelica Root and Sandalwood chips in a muslin bag inside the house near the front door to repel both evil people and evil spirits. Then mix Sandalwood powder with Angelica Root powder and sprinkle the mix across the front of your house.

GRAINS OF PARADISE HOME PROTECTION PACKETS
In New Orleans, conjures used to sew small cloth packets filled with Grains of Paradise and glue or crochet a holy card of Michæl the Archangel to them. These were sold in pairs, one to be placed at the front door and one at the back door, for the protection of the home.

QUINCE SEEDS FOR PROTECTION FROM HARM
The Quince, a relative of the Pear sometimes called the Golden Apple, used to be quite popular in preserves and jams. It is said that if you carry seven Quince seeds in a red flannel bag at your waist, they will protect you from harm. To protect your home, keep Quince seeds, Grains of Paradise seeds, and Star Anise seeds in a packet inside and above the front door.

FIVE-FINGER GRASS TO PROTECT YOUR HOUSEHOLD
Folks say that if you hang a bag of Five-Finger Grass over the fireplace mantle, hidden behind a picture or a mirror, no one will be able to drive you from your home. Likewise, the bag may be hung over your bed to protect you from evil while you sleep. If you blow out and dry an egg, stuff it with Five-Finger Grass, seal the hole with wax, and keep it hidden in the home, the family will be protected from enemies.

THREE ROOTS TO PROTECT FROM THEFT
If you keep much money in the home, place a folded paper packet of dried and crumbled Gall of the Earth root amongst the bills. Sassafras and Alkanet are suitable substitutes for Gall of the Earth in this spell.

FOR PROTECTION FROM LIGHTNING
A Tobacco sack or muslin bag filled with Chamomile and hung in the roof-rafters of a house or barn will protect it from lightning-strikes.

PEACE AND PROTECTION IN THE HOME
Bore a hole in a Red Onion, fill it with sugar, tie a shoe lace around it, and hide it above the door where folks will walk under it.

PROTECTION AGAINST HARM
Rose hips placed in a red flannel bag with Flax seeds will provide protection from harm, especially any illness directed against your body.

TO PREVENT ENEMIES FROM ENTERING THE HOME
Tie nine equal-length pieces of Devil's Shoe Strings all around, and parallel to, a whole Angelica Root. Neatly wrap and tie the bundle together with white thread, finish it off with nine knots, and place it over the door lintel to guard the house.

WORMWOOD BAG FOR PROTECTION
Carried in a little bag or tied in a handkerchief and hung behind the door, Wormwood protects the home and prevents accidents to yourself or anyone in the family.

SILVER DIME, SATOR SQUARE, AND SATURN SEAL
On one side of a 3" square Post-It note write the SATOR square to keep off evil magic and on the other side copy or draw the Fifth Pentacle of Saturn from the Seals of Solomon, to protect the home. Dress the edge of the paper all the way around with King Solomon Wisdom Oil.

Fold the paper up as a seed packet and slip a silver dime into it along with some Red Pepper seeds and Grains of Paradise. Close the packet and hide it under your doorstep, near the front door of your house, or over your front door lintel, to keep evil people from entering.

SAFE TRAVEL MOJO HANDS

COMFREY ROOT FOR SAFETY WHILE TRAVELLING
Comfrey root wards off the evil of unknown strangers and brings good luck in making travel arrangements. Place the root in a red bag, dress it with Van Van Oil, and keep it on you while on the road.

TO PREVENT CAR ACCIDENTS AND VEHICLE THEFT
If placed in a vehicle, a hand made of Ash Tree leaves, Fern leaves, and Comfrey root is said to protect the car and prevent accidents.

A TRAVELLER'S HAND TO KEEP FROM GETTING LOST
Carry Five-Finger Grass, a piece of Comfrey root, and a small lodestone in a black bag dressed with blended Commanding Oil and Power Oil, and you will never get lost. If you feed the hand with magnetic sand and dress it with Lodestone Oil, you will be directed to sources of money as you travel.

MUGWORT, COMFREY, AND A SAINT FOR SAFE TRAVEL
Worn in the shoes, Mugwort is said to prevent fatigue while walking and to keep off wild beasts and the spirits of evil beings who inhabit forlorn places. A red flannel mojo containing Mugwort, Comfrey root, and a Saint Christopher medal is said to provide safety and protection to those who visit foreign places or venture away from home, and to make journeys more pleasant by eliminating interference in one's travel plans.

FEVERFEW AND COMFREY FOR SAFETY ON THE ROAD
For safety while driving, keep Feverfew, Comfrey root, and Plantain leaves in a bag with a Saint Christopher medal in the glove-box, or hang it from the rear-view mirror.

MOJO TO KEEP A TRAVELLING LOVER SAFE
If you feel that your lover may be harmed while on the road, Ash Tree leaves, an Angelica Root, and a Comfrey root make a nice hand for safety. If you fear your lover may be tempted to stray from you sexually while travelling, use the same items, but also add Mugwort, Stay With Me Incense, Return To Me Incense, and a metal anchor charm.

TO BRING YOUR SPOUSE SAFELY HOME

If your husband or wife leaves on a trip, walk behind and lift one of his or her left foot tracks, pulling it out of the dirt from the toe toward the heel, back towards you. Mix it with an equal volume of salt, sew it into a flat cloth packet, and wear it under your left armpit, next to your skin, where you will sweat on it, until your mate returns.

STATE QUARTER "TRIP-TICKET" MOJO

If your trip will take you out of state, obtain a U.S. State Quarter for each state you will go through or fly over. Stack them in the order of your trip, from the State Quarter of your origin to the State Quarter of your destination. On a piece of brown paper bag paper, write out Psalms 121, The Traveller's Psalm *("The Lord will watch over your coming and going …")*. If you only have a few coins, cut the paper square and fold the coins into it, seed-packet style. If you have many coins, cut a rectangle and roll the stacked coins up tightly, tucking in the ends as you would when making a coin roll for the bank. Carry the coin-packet in your purse, glove compartment, or luggage.

PLANTAIN ROOT TO PREVENT VEHICLE THEFT

Plantain root (from the Plantago or Goose Grass plant, not from the Banana relative) is carried in the pocket to protect against Snake bite. It is also recommended that the leaves or root be hung in your car, to protect from theft or from jealous and evil people who envy your fortune.

DEACON MILLETT'S SEVEN-WAY SAFE TRAVEL HAND

This mojo comes from Deacon Millett of FourAltars.com:

"You will need a Comfrey root and six small charms or amulets. They can be made of metal or stone, and they can come from any culture. Some that I have used are a Saint Christopher medal, a Ganesha charm, a tiny jade Kwan Yin carving, an Indian Head penny, a Mercury dime, a hamsa hand, and an anchor.

"Next choose one of these oils or create a blend: Safe Travel Oil, Saint Christopher Oil, Road Opener Oil, Ganesha Oil, Law Keep Away Oil, or, if for a travelling friend or lover, Return To Me Oil.

"Anoint the Comfrey root with your oil, place it in a flannel bag and add the six charms to make a total of seven items as you say Psalms 23, Psalms 27, or your favourite of the various Irish or Saint Patrick prayers."

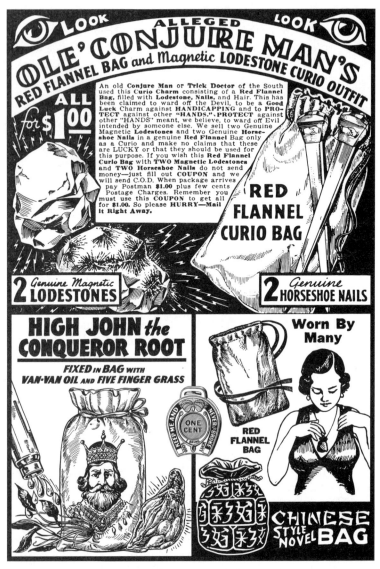

Mojo bags, herbs, minerals, talismans, and oils offered in mail order hoodoo catalogues, 1925 - 2018. Art by Charles C. Dawson, Grey Townsend, and J. C. Strong for Famous Products, King Novelty, J. C. Strong, and the Lucky Mojo Curio Co.

THE HAND OF LOVE

CARRYING A MOJO FOR RELATIONSHIPS

Love-drawing mojos come in as many types as there are types of love. Among the most popular are hands carried to attract social attention, to get offers to date, to encourage casual sex hookups, and to draw declarations of romantic regard. Also important in love work are hands to increase libido, nature, and sexual stamina, both for men and women. Mojos crafted to bring about a proposal of marriage, to celebrate a wedding, to ensure stable fidelity, and to maintain a happy family home may be kept in the bedroom. The nation sack and jack ball are in one sense "power" mojos, but in another sense they are "libido" hands, and so they are included in this section. And, finally, when a relationship crumbles, carrying a mojo may help efforts to rebuild the love that once was shared.

In this chapter you will find mojo hands that will:

- **Attract flirtations, friendships, social enjoyment, and dates.**
- **Cause a new lover to appear in one's life and approach one.**
- **Entice a stranger to engage in sex.**
- **Entice a person who is "just a friend" to desire sex.**
- **Attract romantic partners of the same, opposite, or any gender.**
- **Influence a former lover to return from a distance.**
- **Influence an angry ex-lover to forgive and reconcile.**
- **Influence a steady date to desire to live together or to marry.**
- **Influence a live-in lover to propose marriage.**
- **Take off a jinx that has had a negative effect on one's love-life.**

MINERALS FOR RELATIONSHIPS

Here is a list of minerals included in the protective mojos in this chapter:

- **Lodestones:** The drawing power of strong love; magnetic attraction.
- **Magnetic Sand:** To feed lodestones; energizing sexual power.
- **Matched Coins:** From the lovers' birth years; inscribed with initials.
- **Silver "Mercury" Dime:** For good fortune in luck and love.

HERBS AND ROOTS FOR LOVE AND SEX

Here is a list of herbs and roots included in romance and love mojos:

- **Adam and Eve Roots:** Male and female power; endangered species.
- **Althæa:** To attract helper spirits, heal and soothe, and find a lover.
- **Ash Tree Leaves:** To attract romance and love in a graceful way.
- **Balm of Gilead Buds:** An acceptable substitute for Adam and Eve Roots.
- **Basil:** For peace and joy within the home and family.
- **Blood Root (Coon Root) chips:** For sexual, family-oriented love.
- **Bo' Hog (Lovage) Root:** For luck in love, passion, and sexuality.
- **Calamus Root:** To bring a partner or lover under your command.
- **Cardamom seeds:** For love, sexuality, and charismatic attraction.
- **Catnip:** To entice and charm someone to desire you.
- **Cedar Wood:** For home building, domestic stability, and lusty love.
- **Cherry Bark:** For love, passion, and sexual seductiveness.
- **Cinnamon:** To rapidly attract luck, money, love, and protection.
- **Clover Flowers, Red:** For wholesome, sincere, gentle romance.
- **Cloves:** To attract good luck to your home; to sustain friendships.
- **Cubeb Berries:** To cause your chosen partner or spouse to love you.
- **Damiana:** To arouse passionate, sensual, lustful feelings.
- **Deer's Tongue Leaves:** For a beautiful voice and convincing speech.
- **Dill Seeds:** To draw love close; for family harmony and for babies.
- **Elecampane:** An ingredient in True Love Powder for sincere love.
- **Fig Roots:** For a stable domestic partnership.
- **Gentian Root:** For good luck in matters of love and romance.
- **Ginger:** To spice up and heat up a slow-moving love affair.
- **Ginseng (Wonder of the World) Root:** To empower men sexually.
- **Grains of Paradise:** For good luck in matters of love and romance.
- **Honey:** Used to "glue" photos face-to-face for use in a love mojo.
- **Hyssop:** For forgiveness of any wrong you did; for reconciliation.
- **Jasmine Flowers:** For luck in romance; for thrilling love dreams.
- **John the Conqueror Root:** For personal power and sexual nature.
- **Johnny Jump-Up:** For increasing the speed of a man's sexual arousal.
- **Juniper Berries:** For lusty love and spicy romance.
- **Lavender:** For friendship and love; popular for same-sex love.
- **Lemon Balm:** For a secret affair with a married man.

- **Licorice:** To dominate, rule, or control a lover.
- **Life Everlasting:** For permanence, health, and stability.
- **Mace:** Popular with sex workers and daring women who take chances.
- **Maidenhair Fern:** To attract and secure the love of a woman.
- **Male Fern:** To attract and secure the love of a man.
- **Mandrake Root, American:** For informational dreams about a lover.
- **Mint:** To clear off any difficulties; to protect love and keep it safe.
- **Mistletoe:** An ingredient in True Love Powder for sincere, honest love.
- **Mustard Seeds, White or Yellow:** For blessings and dreams of love.
- **Queen Elizabeth Root:** Grants sexual vitality and power to women.
- **Orange Flowers:** A traditional flower of wedding wreaths.
- **Patchouli:** For love-drawing and money-drawing, and to break jinxes.
- **Periwinkle:** To cause a couple to remain faithful and stay at home.
- **Rattlesnake Master:** To overcome the damage caused by a bad affair.
- **Rose Buds:** For new love, new opportunities, or romance.
- **Rose Petals:** For romance, love, passion, beauty, family.
- **Rosemary:** To give a woman rulership and dominion in her home.
- **Sampson Snake Root:** To give power and strength, especially to men.
- **Self-Heal (All-Heal):** To heal oneself from a past heartbreak.
- **Senna Leaves:** To clear out past influences and prepare for new ones.
- **Skullcap:** To encourage fidelity; for gifts and favours.
- **Southern John (Dixie John) Root:** For contentment within the family.
- **Spikenard:** An ingredient in True Love Powder for sincere, honest love.
- **Sugar:** To sweeten those who might not always express love kindly.
- **Tonka Beans:** To make love-wishes come true; for money in love.
- **Unicorn Root:** For male sexuality and irresistible attractiveness.
- **Violet Leaf:** To ease a broken heart and help in the search for new love.

INCENSE RESINS USED IN LOVE MOJOS

- **Benzoin:** To take off jinxes that have affected your sexual health.
- **Camphor:** To drive off unwanted love-rivals and intruders.
- **Dragon's Blood:** To draw luck and favour in love and romance.
- **Frankincense:** For spiritual blessings in love and family life.
- **Myrrh:** For the development of dreamy sexuality and pleasure.
- **Pine Resin (Rosin):** For restoration after a negative spiritual attack.
- **Sandalwood:** To strengthen the spirit and remove negative conditions.

DRESSING OR FEEDING A LOVE MOJO

- **Adam and Eve Oil:** For a primal love that is fated or destined.
- **Attraction Oil:** To get the attention of those who interest you.
- **Blessing Oil:** For new ventures, new homes, and healing.
- **Bewitching Oil:** For enchantment and sorcerous seduction.
- **Chuparrosa (Hummingbird) Oil:** For a sincere and lasting love.
- **Cleo May Oil:** Used by women for tips, money, and favours from men.
- **Come To Me Oil:** To draw someone to you mentally or physically.
- **Commanding Oil:** To lead others in the paths you prepare for them.
- **Dove's Blood Oil:** For love, and to signify the sealing of a pact.
- **Essence Of Bend-Over Oil:** To impose your will upon others.
- **Fire of Love Oil:** To heat up a love affair, for sexual passion.
- **Follow Me Boy Oil:** To make a man follow you like a dog.
- **Follow Me Girl Oil:** To make a woman follow you like a dog.
- **Hoyt's Cologne:** For luck; its Orange scent signifies marriage.
- **I Dominate My Man Oil:** To gain mental control over a male.
- **I Dominate My Woman Oil:** To gain mental control over a female.
- **Jezebel Oil:** Used by prostitutes to attract wealthy customers.
- **King Solomon Wisdom Oil:** For the author of the Song of Songs.
- **Kiss Me Now! Oil:** For immediate, pleasurable sexual gratification.
- **Lavender Love Drops Oil:** To attract a lover of the same sex.
- **Look Me Over Oil:** To draw attention while out among strangers.
- **Love Me Oil:** For deep, abiding, sincere love that stands the test of time.
- **Marriage Oil:** For a proposal or to strengthen a marriage.
- **Nature Oil:** To enhance sexual libido and stamina in a man.
- **Peaceful Home Oil:** For a blessed and satisfying family life.
- **Power Oil:** For a man's sexual control and his power over women.
- **Q Oil:** To find passion and love with a person of the same sex.
- **Queen Elizabeth Root Oil:** For women's sexual vitality and power.
- **Reconciliation Oil:** To forgive and forget the past; to reunite.
- **Return To Me Oil:** To bring back a lover who has walked out.
- **Sexual Fluids, Menstrual blood:** To mark a partner as one's own.
- **Stay At Home Oil:** To keep a mate home; to reduce running around.
- **Stay With Me Oil:** To stabilize a marriage and prevent a divorce.
- **Van Van Oil:** To clear away negativity and change bad luck to good.
- **Whiskey:** Four Roses for love, Southern Comfort for a happy home.

ATTRACTION AND LOVE-DRAWING HANDS

WISHING AND DREAMING OF NEW LOVE
Carry White Mustard seed, Mandrake Root, Sandalwood, and a pinch of Love Me Sachet Powder to aid the development of love. Sleep with the bag under your pillow to receive information in dreams that will lead to love.

VIOLET LEAVES TO DRAW NEW LOVE
Many people place a Violet leaf in a paper packet in their shoe and wear it that way for seven days, in the belief that they will find a new lover. To do a triple-strength job, some folks use three Violet leaves and wear them seven days each, for a total of twenty-one days, to attract love and romance.

BO' HOG ROOT TO ATTRACT A NEW LOVER
To draw a new lover or increase passion in someone special, carry a red flannel bag in which you have placed three slices of Bo' Hog Root, some Sampson Snake Root, and a whole John the Conqueror Root, if you are male, or a Queen Elizabeth Root, if you are female. Pass it over the flame of a red seven-day candle dressed with Attraction Oil.

CARDAMOM TO ATTRACT A NEW LOVER
Some folks make up a red flannel conjure bag with Cardamom seeds and love-drawing herbs, such as Rose buds, Cubebs, Damiana, or Juniper berries, dressed with Attraction Oil, so that when they meet someone whom they desire, the person they want can be easily led into lust.

ASH TREE LEAVES TO ATTRACT LOVE
Mix Ash Tree leaves with Lavender flowers, Rose buds, and Red Clover, dress with Attraction Oil, and carry in a pink mojo bag.

A QUEEN ELIZABETH ROOT MOJO TO DRAW LOVE
Dress a whole Queen Elizabeth Root with any Orange-scented perfume (such as Hoyt's Cologne) or with Love Me Oil or Come To Me Oil. For flirtation and friendship, add a pinch each of Rose petals, Cloves, Lavender, and Red Clover. For sexual passion and seduction add a pinch each of Patchouli, Damiana, Cherry bark, and Catnip. Carry the root and herbs knotted up in a white cotton handkerchief. Add scent to it as needed.

A TONKA BEAN LOVE-WISHING MOJO

On a small piece of paper, write out your three wishes for love. For instance, you might name three prospective partners *("Manny, if you love me, tell me so," "Moe, if you love me, tell me so," "Jack, if you love me, tell me so")*. If you already have one person in mind, you may name three stages of love *("Jack will ask me for a date," "Jack will give me a kiss," "Jack and i will share a night of passion")*. Name three Tonka Beans after the three wishes *("You are Manny; You are Moe"* or *"You are a kiss; You are a date,"* and so forth). Place the folded paper and the three Tonka Beans in a red flannel bag with a pinch each of Coriander seeds and Rose petals. If you can get the hair of your loved one(s), adding it will strengthen the bag.

TO DRAW ONE WHO IS UNAWARE OF YOUR INTEREST

Write the person's name on paper with Dove's Blood Ink, and put it in a red flannel bag with Senna leaves, Cinnamon chips, and Lovage Root. Dress it with Come To Me Oil, and carry it on your person.

TO SEDUCE A NEW LOVER

Carry Cubebs and Sampson Snake Root in a red bag, and when you meet someone new whom you desire, get one of his or her hairs, put it in the bag, dress it with Love Me Oil, and the one you want will be easily led into love.

MALE FERN ENVELOPE TO ATTRACT A MAN

To draw a man's love, folks have been known to write his name on paper, put it into a small envelope with Male Fern, and carry it in a purse.

A WOMAN'S CHARM TO ATTRACT A MAN'S LOVE

Dress Adam and Eve Roots (or Balm of Gilead Buds) with Adam and Eve Oil, place them in a red flannel bag dressed with Attraction Oil or Come To Me Oil, and wear a little Adam and Eve Oil every day. This will draw a lover to you. If you know the one you want to draw, write a name paper in red ink on parchment, adding his birthdate if possible. Anoint the paper with your urine, and place the parchment in the bag along with the roots.

TO DRAW A MARRIED LOVER FOR A SECRET AFFAIR

Add Lemon Balm to any love-attracting mojo of your choice if you want to attract a married man who will carry on a secret affair with you.

A MAN'S MOJO FOR MORE SEX

Men who want to be always ready to please a woman when she requests sex and men who want more sexual activity, whether from their spouse or from the women they date, can mix Johnny Jump-Up leaves with High John the Conqueror Root chips, Sampson Snake Root chips, and Life Everlasting, then add three Tonka Beans dressed with their own semen and carry them in a red bag dressed with John the Conqueror Oil.

TO ENHANCE MALE NATURE

A red flannel bag containing Sampson Snake Root, High John the Conqueror Root, and Bo' Hog Root dressed with Commanding Oil and Power Oil is said to significantly enhance a man's animal appeal to women. These same three roots, chipped or powdered, can be added to the oil blend and left to steep for a month. The enhanced oil, when rubbed on a man's privates before he has sex, is said to give him more physical energy and control during the act, as well as bringing his partner under his command.

A WOMAN'S BOSOM SACHET TO INCREASE LOVE

Place one Adam root and one Eve root (or a pair of Balm of Gilead Buds), a pair of lodestone grits dressed with magnetic sand, and a mated pair of Blood Root chips (a "He" [brown] and a "She" [pink] chip) all together in a small red flannel bag. Write your lover's name on a small paper in red ink, cross your name over it, and add that to the bag. Feed this hand by sprinkling a pinch of Attraction Powder and a pinch of Love Me Powder into it every morning. Because the items are small, the bag can be worn in a woman's bra, allowing the powders to sift through the cloth slowly to act as a perfume — hence this type of conjure bag used to be called a "bosom sachet." If you like the scent of Lavender, Rose, or Patchouli, these may be added singly or in combination to give an herbal fragrance to the sachet.

MALE-AND-MAIDEN FERN MOJO FOR CONJUGAL LOVE

Mix Male Fern and Maiden Hair Fern in a red conjure bag with two small lodestone pieces, a hair from each person, and a small piece each of High John the Conqueror Root and Queen Elizabeth Root. (In the old days, a pair of Adam and Eve Roots would have been used instead, but they are endangered species now.) Feed the lodestone in the bag with magnetic sand, tie it up, and dress it with Love Me Oil.

SAMPSON SNAKE ROOT FOR A MAN TO ATTRACT LOVE

Sampson Snake Root is generally considered a strengthening "male" root when used in love charms. It is wrapped in a piece of red flannel along with the name paper of the person whose love you desire.

LUCKY LOVE MOJO

If you have recently hooked up with someone and want some luck in getting closer, carry Gentian root chips, Cherry bark, and Dill seeds in a red conjure bag with the name paper and a hair of the beloved, plus at least two other love herbs, such as Rose buds, Queen Elizabeth Root, Lavender, Red Clover, Damiana, Elecampane, Mistletoe, Spikenard, or Catnip. Dress the bag with Love Me Oil and Good Luck Oil.

FOR MEN'S LOVE AFFAIRS

Unicorn Root aids men in love affairs, but only a whole, unbroken root may be employed — and since these are unobtainable in commerce, they must be dug in the wild by the prospective users. Men carry Unicorn Root in a conjure bag to enhance virility and to draw love from a woman. Once they have the woman's love, they may hide the root in her bureau drawer or her closet among her clothing, and she will continue to love them so long as the root remains undisturbed and in place. To keep a male lover faithful, some gay men bind two whole Unicorn roots together tightly with thread and dress them daily with Stay With Me Oil.

TO CHANGE YOUR LUCK IN LOVE

If you have had hard luck in love and want to change it, take a spiritual bath in milk, honey, Cubebs, Violet leaves, and Rose petals, and then carry a mojo bag containing Rattlesnake Master root, Lovage root, High John the Conqueror Root, a single lodestone, magnetic sand, and a silver dime, dressed with Hoyt's Cologne and Van Van Oil.

FOR A SPICY, HEATED LOVE

If you are in a slow-moving love affair with a cautious man and want to heat things up and hurry him along toward a more sexually driven relationship, carry a mojo made with Jasmine, Ginseng, Grains of Paradise, Ginger, Cinnamon, Mace, and Rose buds. Dress the bag with a blend of Bewitching Oil and Fire of Love Oil.

AN INCENSE-BASED MOJO FOR LOVE

This mojo is unusual in that all of the ingredients can be burned as incense. You can make twice as much as you need for your conjure hand and burn the rest on charcoal to smoke and fix the bag. Mix equal parts by weight of Patchouli, Damiana, Benzoin, Camphor, Dragon's Blood, Frankincense, Myrrh, Pine Resin, Sandalwood, and Fire of Love Incense.

DRAGON'S BLOOD MOJO HAND FOR LOVE

A chunk of Dragon's Blood resin carried in a red flannel bag with at least two love herbs and dressed with Love Me Oil is lucky for love.

A WOMAN'S CHARM FOR A PROPOSAL OF MARRIAGE

Place a pair of Adam and Eve roots (or two Balm of Gilead Buds) in a red flannel bag dressed with Love Me Oil, and tuck it into your lover's pocket on the night of the full moon. He will propose marriage to you within two weeks. Depending on how well you and he agree on the subject of matrimony, you may do this with his knowledge, or when he is not looking.

A MAN'S CHARM FOR PROPOSAL OF MARRIAGE

If a man carries Deer's Tongue leaf wrapped in red silk inside a red flannel bag, he will be able to talk his woman into marrying him.

SOUTHERN JOHN MARRIAGE MOJO

Put a whole Southern John Root in a red flannel bag with a pinch of Violet leaves and a pinch of lodestone grit dressed with magnetic sand. Dress the bag with Hoyt's Cologne and Stay With Me Oil. If you and your mate have been fighting, substitute Peaceful Home Oil or mix the two.

FROM GIRLFRIEND TO WIFE

Get toenail clippings from all ten of your woman's toes by asking to cut her nails. Put these in a packet with hair from her right armpit. and three Black-Eyed Peas. Carry the packet in your pocket, and within two weeks, she will accept your marriage proposal.

TO BRING BACK A DRIFTING LOVER

Carry Damiana and Balm of Gilead Buds with your straying lover's personal concerns in a flannel bag, so that he or she will return to you.

DOUBLE-LODESTONE MOJOS FOR LOVE

BASIC DOUBLE LODESTONE MOJO HAND FOR LOVE
A matched pair of pebble-sized lodestones fed with magnetic sand is a classic basis for a love hand. Add personal concerns and herbs appropriate to the condition being addressed. Carry these in red flannel, dressed with Hoyt's Cologne, Attraction Oil, or Come To Me Oil; wear it in a front pocket, near the genitals. When you attract someone, fold your hairs and theirs into a paper on which you have written your lover's name three times crossed by your name written three times. There are many variations, but here are a few i like:

DOUBLE LODESTONE HAND FOR A SEXUAL ENCOUNTER
Start with the basic double-lodestone bag and add Spikenard, Rose buds, Calamus, Damiana, and Juniper berries. Dress the bag with your own sexual fluids and Kiss Me Now! Oil. When you attract someone, add their personal concerns and sexual fluids, and dress it with Follow Me Boy (or Girl) Oil.

DOUBLE LODESTONE HAND FOR SAME-SEX LOVE
Start with the basic double-lodestone bag and add Safflower petals, Lavender flowers, Sampson Snake Root, and Rose buds. Dress the bag with your own sexual fluids and Lavender Love Drops Oil. When you attract someone, add their personal concerns and their sexual fluids.

DOUBLE LODESTONE HAND FOR OPPOSITE-SEX LOVE
Start with the basic double-lodestone bag and add Cubebs, Damiana, and Rose petals. Dress the bag with your own sexual fluids and Love Me Oil. When you attract someone, add their personal concerns and sexual fluids.

DOUBLE LODESTONE HAND FOR A DEEP RELATIONSHIP
Start with the basic double-lodestone bag and add a matched pair of Balm of Gilead Buds, a matched pair of John the Conqueror Roots for two males, a matched pair of Queen Elizabeth Roots for two females, or one John the Conqueror and one Queen Elizabeth root for a male-female couple. Dress the bag with your own sexual fluids and Stay With Me Oil. When you attract someone, add their personal concerns and their sexual fluids. This bag can be turned into a marriage-drawing hand by beginning with the extra addition of Deer's Tongue leaves and dressing the bag with Marriage Oil.

"FEED THE HE, FEED THE SHE": A HAND MADE IN A SOCK

In 1928 Ruth Mason of New Orleans, Louisiana, shared this hand with the folklorist Zora Neale Hurston: "Get his sock. Take one silver dime, some hair from his head or his hatband. Lay the sock out on a table, bottom up. Write his name three times and put it on the sock. Place the dime on the name and the hair or hatband on the dime. Put a piece of 'he' lodestone on top of the hair and sprinkle it with steel dust. As you do this, say, 'Feed the he, feed the she.' That is what you call feeding the lodestone. Then fold the sock heel on the toe and roll it all up together tight. Pin the bundle by crossing two needles. Then wet it with whiskey and set it up over a door."

Ruth Mason's used one lodestone and one sock — the man's. I learned a variant in Oakland, California, in the 1960s, from a man who had come to the East Bay from Louisiana. He had two large lodestones on a work bench for clients. One was the "he" and one the "she." He named and trained lodestone grits or magnetic Scotty Dog charms by setting them as "riders" on the large tones. He used one sock from the man and one from the woman and inserted the named Scotty Dog or grit into its owner's sock with a name slip the size of a Chinese fortune cookie paper. Then he rolled the socks together, as if they were a pair, turned his client's end over the rollto hold it, and stuck two needles through, to make a cross. This was buried.

Magnetic Scotty dogs being trained as "riders" on a matched pair of lodestones fed for love. They can be carried in a mojo or rolled in socks as described above. Art by Charles C. Dawson and Grey Townsend for King Novelty and Lucky Mojo Curio Co.

BED AND MATTRESS PACKETS FOR LOVE

HIDDEN LOVE HANDS FOR THE BED
Love hands may be hidden under the bed, between slats and springs, between springs and mattress, or a mattress seam may be opened, the packet inserted, and the seam sewed shut. You can hide them in pillows as well.

BED PACKET FOR WOMEN WHO WANT TO DRAW MEN
Mix Catnip, Raspberry leaf, and Rosemary to attract the man (or men) you want. Use half the mix to make a tea-bath, and roll the rest in your underwear, dressed with your menstrual blood or a drop of urine. Hide this in your bed, and sprinkle a bit of your used bath water at the corners of the bed.

ENHANCING SEX IN A MARRIAGE
Blood Root chips that are pinkish are called "Queens" or "She roots" and those that are dark red-brown are called "Kings" or "He roots." Wrap a King root chip and a Queen root chip, dressed with Love Me Oil, in red flannel, and sew it into the mattress to keep things happy between "He" and "She."

BED PACKET TO BIND A LOVER TO YOU
"Glue" a photo of you and one of your lover face-to-face with honey. Place this on a red cloth, with Knot Weed, Periwinkle, Rose petals, Calamus, Licorice, and Love Me Powder. Fold the cloth, tie it up with your shoelaces, dress it with Love Me Oil, and keep it under your bed. To call an absent love back, use Return To Me Powder and Oil instead and bury it at your doorstep.

SPANISH BONE PACKET FOR THE BED
If a man wishes to gain the love of a woman, he gives her a Racoon love bone as a token of his esteem, or buries such a bone beneath her doorstep or in her yard. Among married couples this so-called Spanish bone is dressed with sexual fluids, then rolled up tightly in a piece cut from the man's unwashed underwear, and placed beneath the bed to aid in satisfying conjugal relations.

BED PACKET FOR MARRIED COUPLES
To enhance a marriage, put two lodestones, two Balm of Gilead Buds, a paired John the Conqueror Root and Queen Elizabeth Root, and two Rose buds in a small bag and hide it beneath the bed.

PERIWINKLE FOR LOVE IN MARRIAGE
Periwinkle leaves are sewn into the mattress to keep husband and wife forever in love, in a peaceful home, and always faithful.

MAGNOLIA IN THE MATTRESS TO HOLD A MAN
Fold a pair of Magnolia leaves into a white handkerchief and either sew them in the mattress or lay them flat between the box springs and mattress. They will dry naturally. After you do this, steep a handful of dried Raspberry leaves in a quart of boiling water. Strain, cool, and pour it over your body while speaking aloud the name of your mate. A man will never want to wander or stray far from home if his wife bathes her genitals in Raspberry leaf tea, so catch that Raspberry tea-bath and use it to launder your bed linens — and you will have made your bed just right.

FOR A HAPPY AND SEXUALLY FULFILLING MARRIAGE
Take one of your socks and one of your mate's socks, tie them in a knot, and hide them under the bed. If you put one of each partner's hairs in his and her respective socks before you tie the knot, it will be stronger.

TO KEEP LOVE LONG AND STRONG
Dress two Adam and Eve Roots with Stay With Me Oil, and place each one in a red flannel bag. If you can't get Adam and Eve Roots, use two Balm of Gilead Buds, two Coon Roots, and two name papers. Put a lodestone grit dressed with magnetic sand in each bag, plus a John the Conqueror Root for the "He" bag and a Queen Elizabeth Root for the "She" bag. The man carries the Eve bag and the woman carries the Adam bag when they are apart, and this will keep their love long and strong. When they are in the same house, the two bags are tied together by their strings and kept under the bed.

TO KEEP YOUR SPOUSE SEXUALLY SATISFIED AT HOME
Get a personal concern of your mate's, such as a hair, and place it at the center of a bundle of Patchouli leaf. If the man has trouble performing sexually, hide a Raccoon penis bone in the center of the bundle. If the woman is not sexually responsive, a dressed Cowrie shell goes in the center. Wrap and tie the bundle tightly with red thread, finish it with nine knots, and sprinkle it with a mixture of Love Me Oil and Stay With Me Oil and hide it beneath the bed, under the slats or in the mattress.

ROSEMARY BED PACKET FOR A FAITHFUL MARRIAGE

If a married woman carries Rosemary in a blue flannel bag with a whole Angelica Root, it is said that she will be the dominant partner and that there will be peace in the home and faithfulness in the marriage. In addition, Rosemary is one of the "bed herbs" — herbs commonly sewn into a flat red flannel packet which is in turn sewn inside the mattress for fidelity and a happy home. A bed herb packet may contain three, seven, or nine of the following herbs: Rosemary, a pair of Balm of Gilead Buds, a small Angelica root, Lavender flowers, Rose petals, Coriander seed, Cumin seed, Periwinkle leaves, and whole Magnolia leaves.

BED AND KITCHEN BOTTLE TO FORCE A MARRIAGE

Get a hair from the mould of your lover's head and one of his or her pubic hairs; put them in a small wide-mouthed bottle with a silver dime. Pray over it for a marriage and hide it under the bed, then make love over it. After that, capture some of your combined sexual fluids on a piece of cloth or paper, let it dry out, and add that to the bottle; fill the bottle with sugar, and keep it under the bed for one month. If you do not receive any indication that a marriage will be forthcoming, take the bottle out from under the bed and use the sugar in cooking for one month, a little bit at a time. When the sugar is all gone, your last chance to force a marriage will come if you bury the bottle beneath your kitchen back steps and leave it there for a month. If this does not work, you may have chosen the proverbial "wrong man," and should try some binding spells.

PEACEFUL HOME HERBS UNDER THE BED

Mixtures that contain herbs such as Periwinkle, Basil, Rosemary, Borage, and Balm of Gilead Buds, dressed with Peaceful Home and Stay With Me Oils, are often sold under the name Peaceful Home Herb Mix. To improve conjugal relations, ensure fidelity, put an end to domestic disputes, and soothe family troubles, carry this mix in a flannel bag or, better yet, put it in a muslin bag and hide the bag under the bed. Make love on the bed and feed the bag with your combined sexual fluids. Do this at least three times. Then, with the herbs still in the bag, brew it inboiling water to make a tea, and use that to make a floor wash. Rise before dawn, scrub the home from front to back as you pray for happiness to enter the home, and throw the left-over leaves toward the rising sun.

THE NATION SACK

INFORMANT #1517: "THE NATION SACK WOMAN"

What follows is an extract from a long interview that Harry Hyatt conducted with a woman he recorded as Informant #1517 in October, 1939, in Memphis, Tennessee. Hyatt described her as "a hoodoo woman ... a small-time worker or occasional worker" — by which he meant that she made conjurations for others, but was not a full-time professional at the trade. Hyatt, who did not reveal the names of his informants, said, "I have called her 'The Nation Sack Woman' because at the end of the interview she gave me an excellent account of the nation sack or nation bag — a fetish to some women and worn by them." I believe she revealed that her name was Mrs. Simpson.

My comments are [in brackets].

HUNG BELOW THE WAIST, NOT TO BE TOUCHED

"The nation bag — they make this bag around — a belt around them, and that bag hangs right down here, and they tote their money and all their different little concerns like I'm telling you about."

[What she has been telling him about are numerous hoodoo spells that utilize bluestone, sugar, nails, lodestones, salt, urine, photographs, hair, a person's name written on paper, and so forth. Thus, these "different little concerns" are the physical objects women use in hoodooing.]

"They tote some of the men's concernings [that is, personal physical objects such as the man's fingernail clippings, pubic hair, a nine-knot string charm with the man's nature or name tied into it, or a fragment of cloth soiled with his semen] — they got it in that bag. You know, a man better not try to put their hand on that bag; you know, he better not touch. He going, 'cause when she pulls it off at night — if she sleeps by herself, she sleeps with it on; but if she got a husband, you'll see her every night go and lock it up in that trunk. Next morning you see her go there and get it. He never touch it — she got her stuff in there. All of her stuff, that's where she tote that. She got her money in there and her snuffbox and all that other stuff — you say 'tobies' — that's what's in that bag. [It appears that Hyatt had asked her if she knew about tobies, and she responded by describing nation sacks.]

"And don't you touch that bag. If you [a man] want to have some serious trouble — probably make him get sick [with unnatural illness]."

MRS. SIMPSON'S SECRET

"My husband's mother, she was a real old lady, about 95 years old. She had a bag on her and I'm the one that fetched it 'cause she drew pensions, and I'm the one got her money out 'cause I had to take care of it, and so she had more different little — I don't know, different little [things] tied up.

"I know she did conjuring on Mr. Simpson, her husband, for years, 'cause she had married him, I imagine, fifty years old, and she really kept him, too. She had him in that bag, in her nation sack."

[If Mrs. Simpson died at age 95, before Hyatt conducted this interview in 1939, she would have to have been born before 1844. Additionally, the informant was subtly telling Hyatt something he did not pick up on — that although men cannot touch a nation sack, old Mrs. Simpson readily let her daughter-in-law — *another woman* — handle it.]

"She had that nation sack and done wore it, and she sewed. She had so much confidence in that [sack] that she wouldn't throw it away. She sewed it to another brand-new one, and that wore out, put that in another one — her nation sack was that big [demonstrates].

"My husband, he say, "My mother wouldn't never let you touch that," say, "My daddy never has had his hands on that nation sack."

[Hyatt failed to note that the informant's husband was wrong — his mother did let her handle the nation sack. She implied that the taboo is only against men touching it, and men are not always aware of the gender bias in the taboo.]

Hyatt asked, "Do women still wear them as much as they used to?"

"Well, now, when you find one that's accustomed to things like that. I know several women who wears them, women that have got to wear them now. In wearing that junk [conjure charms] on them, they've got to have a nation sack, see. And if they've got a man sleeping with them, done got heaps of these things, and they can't have these things around them untied."

[Many hoodoo spells involve folding, wrapping, tying, sewing, or placing objects in a cloth; "untied" objects would be liable to be touched or seen.]

"They [the men] want to know what's it about. And when they [the women] get it [roots, charms, and personal concerns of the man] covered down in that nation sack, see, they pull it off [themselves at night] and lock it up, see, 'cause nobody is supposed to touch it. And when they get up in the morning, they put it on, and then they can't get [back] in the bed. Well, you see, they're afraid they might go to sleep [in the bed], and he [the man might] examine it, you know. There's lots of them. I know several of us wearing them."

MY OWN NATION SACK TO CONTROL A MAN

Get a dime from each of your birth-years, a saucer, a small red candle, and something personal of the man you love and want. Write his name 9 times on a piece of paper. If you can get his handwriting, add that too, because he touched it. If you know him well, then get his personal, biological concerns: his hair, his sweat on a scrap of cloth, and, as soon as ever you can, his semen. Place any or all of these under an overturned white saucer with the candle on top. Dress each dime with your menstrual blood and Follow Me Boy Oil, calling them by his and your names, saying *"This is [his name]"* and *"This is [your name]."* Dress a John the Conqueror Root and a Queen Elizabeth Root with your menstrual blood and Follow Me Boy Oil, saying *"This is [his name]"* and *"This is [your name]."* Set his root on his dime and your root on your dime. Place any extra personal items of his in the mojo bag. Dress an empty red flannel bag with Follow Me Boy Oil, stroking it 9 times and saying, *"[Name of lover], follow me."*

Pass the bag through the candle smoke 9 times saying, *"[Name of lover], come to me."* Place the dimes and roots in the bag saying, *"[Name of lover], stay with me."* When the candle is done, take the items from under the saucer and fold the paper toward you, saying *"[Name of lover], follow me"* with every fold. Place it in the Nation Sack, saying, *"[Name of lover], stay with me."* Dispose of any left over candle wax at a crossroads, throwing it to the East (toward sunrise) over your left shoulder and walking away without looking back. From this time onward, carry the Nation Sack on you when you are with him or keep it in your bedroom where he will not see or touch it. Add more personal items to it when you can. Here is the best one of all:

Measure off a length of soft cotton string as long as his erect penis. Tie the beginning of a knot in the center of the string — that is, make the knot but leave it loose. Hide the string under your pillow or in the bathroom. Make love with him but do not come (you want only HIS nature in this charm). Wipe yourself with the string to get his come on it. Now wait until he falls asleep. When he has drifted off, hold the string by the two ends. Call his name, and just as he answers, pull the knot tight. Many women will prefer to put nine knots in a string this way, tying the knots on nine different days, to really hoodoo their man's nature so he cannot ever love another, but one knot is sufficient to start. Place the knotted string in your nation sack and he will always be yours.

GAY AND LESBIAN NATION SACKS

I know several gay men who have made and used a nation sack with good results. This form of mojo hand may have originated as a woman's trick around Memphis, Tennessee, some time in the 19th century, but gay men all around the country certainly have picked up on it by now!

Lesbian women can easily make a nation sack on another woman. To take a woman's measure, mark the length from the clitoral glans to the anus. Use a fairly thin string, because, since the length is shorter than a man's measure, making all those knots would be difficult in thick string.

A MAN CAN MAKE A NATION SACK ON A WOMAN

If a man wanted to make this sort of a trick bag on a woman, he would have to reverse everything — he would put his semen on the coins and anoint the string with her sexual fluids from a union while she was on her period *and* he did not have an orgasm but she did — combining her period blood with her fluids of arousal and thus tying two of her powers (her fascination power and her nature) in the same knots.

One reason this reversal may not be popular with men, though, is that few African-American men will have sex with a woman on her period, so powerful is the bewitching power of her menstrual blood. Most especially, they may refuse oral sex on her at that time — or at any time, for fear of being caught by her if she were to lie and say she was not on her period when she actually was, because once they tasted her menses, they would be tied to her just as sure as if she fed them that stuff in coffee, tea, or spaghetti sauce. And that, in a nutshell, may be why the nation sack is seldom used by men to catch women — it's too risky for men to prepare it!

MENSTRUAL BLOOD ON THE COINS

The reason menstrual blood is put on the coins is to symbolize the woman's sexual and financial power over the man. Most women understand that menstrual blood, because it is so important to our lives and has such a restricted supply — only a few days a month, only a few years out of a woman's life (between menarche and menopause), only when the woman is fertile (not pregnant or nursing) — is the traditional "right" body fluid to use to capture a mate for marriage. Some women never have periods. Some women are too young, too old, have had a hysterectomy, are pregnant, or are nursing, so those women use vaginal fluids or a drop of urine instead.

ARE BIRTH-YEAR COINS ESSENTIAL?

The birth-year coins in a nation sack are primarily a way of identifying each person and having a special link. Most coins only stay in circulation a few years. After that, you have to ask for them by date at a coin shop. You can buy them in "circulated" condition for very little cost.

Some women don't use birth-year coins. Instead, to symbolize the man, they employ a coin of any date or denomination that the man gave them from his own hand. To represent themselves, they may use a lucky coin they found or one that they like for any reason.

If you would rather use bright, shiny, modern coins, or coins from the year that the two of you met or married, then go right ahead. You may keep quite a few coins in a nation sack, including your spending money.

WILL A NATION SACK DRAW A NEW LOVE?

You would generally use the nation sack on a man who is yours, whether you are married to him or not. You need some money he gave you, his semen, his hair or fingernail clippings, and so forth — so a nation sack is typically not used on a man with whom you are not already really close.

WILL A NATION SACK BRING A MARRIED MAN TO ME?

If you are the "outside woman" and your lover's wife is working to hold him, it is unlikely that a nation sack would break them up, although it certainly should make him want to continue seeing you for sex.

STRING WITHOUT THE BAG, BAG WITHOUT THE STRING

The semen on the string is knotted in order for the man's nature to be captured, and the reason for the woman to not have an orgasm at the time she collects the semen is because she wants to have a clear head, to keep her magical intent in mind, and not get captured herself.

Although a nation sack generally does contain a knotted string, there are many other forms of work that employ knotted strings. A knotted string may be used as a candle wick, for instance, and burned to destroy a man's nature. And a nation sack can be made without a knotted string in it.

Nation sacks are different than most other mojo hands for love:

They always contain coins. They can be opened and remade. They generally contain the personal concerns or nature of one's beloved, and this may (or may not) take the form of a knot-spell.

THE JACK BALL

A MAN'S JACK BALL TO ATTRACT WOMEN

To make a luck ball, goofer ball, jack ball, or jack for love, get two small lodestone chips that draw to each other, cover them with magnetic sand, and mould them into a little ball with beeswax. Warm the wax and embed a mixture of small John the Conqueror Root chips, Gentian root chips, and Bo' Hog Root chips into the surface. You can use Pine pitch or tree sap instead of wax, just so you bind the root chips together around the mated lodestones and magnetic sand. Wrap the finished ball with red thread all over, covering every bit over and over until no wax or pitch can be seen. Tie off the thread with nine knots.

If you leave a loop thread from which to hang it, you can use this Jack as a love-divining pendulum to determine how a woman feels about you. Some people make the hanging loop short, as on a pendulum. Others like it long enough to sling it over the shoulder and carry the jack under the left armpit.

You can also "work"or "operate" the suspended jack round and around in ellipses that come toward you, to draw a woman to you, or to push one away.

You may place the jack in a red conjure bag and dress the bag with John the Conqueror Oil when you go out to party and pick up women — but the bag is just to carry it; the jack itself is the charm.

"THREE JOHNS" JACK BALL FOR DIVINATION POWER

Embed small pieces of the three "John Roots" — High John, Dixie John, and Little John — in a tiny chip of beeswax with your own hair and name written on a slip of paper. Wrap the ball round and around with red thread or pearl cotton to make a jack with a loop, and tie it off with nine knots. Carry it in a red bag dressed with High John the Conqueror Oil. Use the jack as a pendulum to divine your own best course of action. It holds a spark of your essence — it's like a little storage battery of YOU — and as long as it is fed, it is ready to work for you, answer your questions, and bring you luck.

A JACK FOR A WOMAN?

I first bought a jack for myself back in the 1960s, and i am a woman, so i would say that whether you want one and will use it depends on how tough a grrrl you are. Some chicks would not wish to carry a jack ball — but most adventurous women i know will and do carry one.

MOJOS FOR FAMILY BLESSINGS

VANDAL ROOT AND LOVAGE TO STOP MARITAL FIGHTING
Wrap Vandal Root and a picture of you and your spouse in brown paper. Carry this packet for three days and then take out the Vandal Root and throw it into running water, to take the fighting away. Replace it with Lovage root and keep that with the picture thereafter.

BASIL FOR HAPPINESS AND PEACE IN THE FAMILY
Basil is a family-protection herb, so when combined with love herbs such as Red Clover, Rose buds, Catnip, Gentian root, Damiana, Lavender, Cubebs, Juniper berries, and Deer's Tongue, it is said to increase affection in the family and keep the home peaceful.

TO BREAK UP SLANDER AGAINST YOUR MARRIAGE
Combine at least three of the following six protective herbs: Slippery Elm bark, Agrimony, Rosemary, Rue, Mint, and Adder's Tongue. Add to them a Cat's Eye shell and a piece of alum and carry this in a toby to break spells involving slander and lies spread by back-biting enemies or jealous in-laws who are trying to trouble your home-life.

TO RULE AND PROTECT YOUR HOME
Tie a mojo bag filled with dried Rosemary leaves over the lintel, and all who pass under it when entering will respect the woman of the home.

BLOOD ROOT TO GAIN RESPECT FOR YOUR MARRIAGE
Tie a red bag filled with Blood Root chips and Rosemary over the lintel, and all who pass under it will respect and acknowledge your marriage.

PEACEFUL HOME, FAITHFUL MARRIAGE
Dress a whole Angelica Root with Peaceful Home Oil, add a pinch of Lavender and a small family photograph, and carry the three items in a blue flannel bag, or place them somewhere under the bed.

FOR PEACE AT HOME WHILE YOU TRAVEL
Dress a Comfrey root with Peaceful Home Oil and carry it while abroad, and you'll return to peace in the home and faithfulness in the marriage.

MOJOS FOR MARITAL FIDELITY

SOCKS TO STOP YOUR PARTNER'S RUNNING AROUND
Get your lover's hair and put it in one of his socks. Use three tacks to fix the sock up under your bed. The open end of the sock points to the head of the bed and the toe to the foot of the bed. If possible, turn the sock so that the toe itself points away from the bedroom door and toward an inside wall.

A FRONT DOOR PACKET TO KEEP YOUR MATE HOME
Get your spouse's hair tie, hair band, or hat bow and tuck three of your own pubic hairs in it. Wrap it in a piece of paper. Dress it with Stay With Me Oil and carefully hide it above the front door where your partner walks under, and he or she will want to stay at home more.

LODESTONES KEEP LOVE ALIVE WHEN YOU TRAVEL
Select two very small lodestones or lodestone chips that make a good pair — when positioned head to tail they should attract strongly and share a snug surface in common. Place them together, feed them with magnetic sand to give them a "hairy" coating, and anoint them with Love Me Oil and your conjoined sexual fluids. Say a prayer for the continuation of your love over long distances, then gently separate the lodestones, keeping as much magnetic sand on them as possible, and place each one in a red flannel bag. Tie the bags shut, and each keep one while you are apart. They will draw you back together again. When the two of you are reunited, complete the ritual by taking the lodestones out and reuniting them, head to tail. Dress them with anointing oil and with your bodily fluids, then feed them with more magnetic sand. Thereafter you may keep the lodestones in a bowl on your altar, or under your bed, or bury them together in your yard.

SEVEN CLOVES FOR THOSE WHO MUST PART
Fill two small bags with seven Cloves each and hang them on cords as necklaces. Add to each bag a coin from the birth year of each person and also add the hairs or fingernails of each person. Feed the bags the first time with the combined sexual fluids of both people, and thereafter feed them with Return To Me Oil and Safe Travel Oil. If the two of you reunite before the cords break and the contents spill, you will know that your lover remained true while you were parted.

MOJOS TO RULE AND CONTROL A LOVER

FIG AND CEDAR TO MAKE A LOVER FOLLOW YOU
Wrap a fresh Fig leaf tightly around a strip of Cedar bark or wood and wrap a paper with Genesis 2:24 (*"Therefore shall a man leave his father and his mother, and shall cleave unto his wife: and they shall be one flesh."*) written on it tightly around them both. Carry this on you, and your lover will follow if you move.

HOYT'S COLOGNE BOTTLE HAND TO RULE YOUR LOVER
Buy a small bottle of Hoyt's Cologne and replace the cap with a cork stopper, through which you have driven nine pins all the way down, so they contact the cologne. Next, cut a small piece from your lover's clothes, and push it to the bottom of the bottle. After that, get some of your lover's fingernails and toenails, which you can do by asking to trim them, or watching carefully when they are being trimmed and finding any that jump or fall away. Put those in the bottle. You now have three personal concerns in there. The next three concerns to add are hairs from three places on your lover's body — head hair, body or armpit hair, and pubic hair. Finally, because there are nine pins in the cork, you need three more personal concerns, namely fluids, such as urine, spit, and semen, menstrual blood, or vaginal fluid (but don't get any of your own stuff mixed up in there!). Once you have exactly nine items in the bottle — three solids, three hairs, and three fluids — top it up again with fresh Hoyt's Cologne if the pins are no longer touching the liquid, and then seal it with wax from a burning red candle dressed with Commanding Oil. When you want to exercise control over your lover, talk to the bottle, saying, *"Now, [Name], do what i say, and come under my command,"* and turn the bottle gently upside-down and rightside-up a few times as you do so. The pain caused by the nine pins coming into contact with the personal concerns will cause your lover to obey your command.

QUASSIA CHIPS FOR A LOVE-CONTROLLING MOJO
Most workers look askance on any attempts at substitution for personal concerns, but some say that if you burn Quassia chips *with* your lover's hair or other concerns and keep the ashes in a black bag in a dark place, you can control your lover.

COUCH GRASS TO DOMINATE A LOVER
Couch Grass or Witch Grass is reputed to attract and dominate a new lover. Those who use it for this purpose wind and wrap it around something personal from their lover then sew it tightly into a piece of chamois leather.

A MAN'S HAND TO MASTER A WOMAN
If your woman is always raising sand, this may be the way to master her. Dress a John the Conqueror Root with Master Oil, I Dominate My Woman Oil, and Commanding Oil. Combine Master Root, Master of the Woods, and Rattlesnake Master, and spit on them. Some say to chew Tobacco and spit, others say to chew Licorice (or even Licorice Whips candy) and spit. In any case, bundle these items up in a leather bag, dress the bag with the combined oils, command her to hold her peace, and wear the bag on you.

A WOMAN'S HAND TO MASTER A MAN
If your man is bad-tempered, this may bring him under your control. Wrap a Queen Elizabeth Root with Rosemary in a piece of cloth cut from his underwear, and dress it with I Dominate My Man Oil. If he won't share his money, beg until you do get a coin, carve on it *"From [His Name] to [Your Name] with Love,"* and wrap that up with the root and the herb.

A LOVE-CONTROLLING MOJO
To get the upper hand in a love affair, wrap Calamus root, Licorice root, and the personal concerns of your lover in a packet and dress the packet with Controlling Oil before putting it into a love-bag.

TO COMMIT ADULTERY WITH IMPUNITY
If you want to cheat on your marriage, but you don't want any objections from your spouse, make a mojo hand with broken pins and needles to symbolize your broken marriage vows. Be sure to break the eyes of the needles so your mate will not see what is going on. Add one of your spouse's pubic hairs and a pinch of Tobacco snuff to dominate your mate, and a pinch of sugar to keep the relationship sweet. If you are a female and your mate is male, add some dried Rosemary. If you are male and your mate is female, add some Master of the Woods leaves. Sew everything up into a tight little packet, wear it next to your skin, and your spouse will not raise a fuss, even if you get caught running around.

MOJOS FOR REUNION OR RECONCILIATION

TO SOOTHE LOVE PROBLEMS
If you have fought with your mate, mix Hyssop, Balm of Gilead Buds, Violet or Pansy leaves, and Self-Heal. Carry this mix in a bag to alleviate the problems, especially if you are sorrowful because you were in the wrong.

TO RESTORE A WIFE'S LOVE
Pick up one of your wife's homeward-bound foot tracks, lifting it from heel to toe to draw her closer. Mix it to the consistency of mud with Hoyt's Cologne, a pinch of crumbled Camphor, and three strands of her head-hair. Sew it into a flat red flannel packet and wear it under your left armpit, in the hairs, to get your armpit sweat on it. You'll soon be happy together again.

TO FOSTER RECONCILIATION
For reconciliation with an estranged lover, friend, or spouse, make a simple reconciliation mojo with something personal of each of you, plus equal parts Balm of Gilead Buds, Rose buds, Althæa, and Lavender flowers. This is a mojo to roll or work, praying for your companion to return. It should be small enough to hold in your hand as you pray.

TO BRING AN ANGRY MAN HOME
If your man has fought with you and walked out in anger, put a hair from his head, a hair from his armpit, and one of his pubic hairs down into the toe of one of his socks. Roll the sock up very tightly toward you, as you wish aloud for him to come back home; he soon will return and you can reconcile.

A SWATCH OF CLOTH TO BRING BACK A LOVER
Deacon Millett shares this one: "An old-time worker in Waycross, Georgia, told Harry Hyatt to cut a one-inch piece from the target's shirt, and baptise it *in your own name*. Then, on a small piece of paper, write your name and the name of your absent lover in red ink, as tiny as you can. Fold the names together and wrap the cloth around them. "Tote it anywhere about you — in your pocketbook, in your shoe. He'll soon return."

For many more ways to get a lover or spouse to come back to you, see:
"Hoodoo Return and Reconciliation Spells" by Deacon Millett

BIBLIOGRAPHY

DE CLAREMONT, Lewis. *Legends of Incense, Herb, and Oil Magic*. Oracle Publishing Co., 1936. Dorene Publishing, 1966. Restored edition, Lucky Mojo Curio Co., 2016.

HOHMAN, [Johann Georg]. *Pow-Wows or The Long Lost Friend*. Stein, 1935. [Reprints *The Long Secreted Friend or A True and Christian Information for Everybody; Containing Wonderful and Approved Remedies and Arts for Men and Beasts*. John George Hohman, 1846]

HURSTON, Zora Neale. *Mules and Men*. J.B. Lippincott, 1935. Harper Perennial, 1990.

HYATT, Harry Middleton. *Hoodoo – Conjuration – Witchcraft – Rootwork*. [Five Vols.] Memoirs of the Alma Egan Hyatt Foundation, 1970-1978.

JOHNSON, F. Roy. *The Fabled Doctor Jim Jordan, a Story of Conjure*. Johnson Publishing Co, 1963.

LAFOREST, Aura. *Hoodoo Spiritual Baths*. Lucky Mojo Curio Co., 2014.

LAFOREST, Aura. *Women's Work: Home-Style Hoodoo Spells for Marriage, Sex, and Motherhood*. Lucky Mojo Curio Co., 2017.

LEFÆ, Miss PHŒNIX. *Cash Box Conjure*. Lucky Mojo Curio Co., 2018.

MATHERS, Samuel Liddell MacGregor. *The Key of Solomon the King (Clavicula Salomonis)*. George Redway, 1888.

MICHÆLE, Miss and Prof. Charles Porterfield. *Hoodoo Bible Magic: Sacred Secrets of Scriptural Sorcery*. Missionary Independent Spiritual Church, 2014.

MILLETT, Deacon. *Hoodoo Honey and Sugar Spells*. Lucky Mojo Curio Co., 2013.

MILLETT, Deacon. *Hoodoo Return and Reconciliation Spells*. Lucky Mojo Curio Co., 2015.

[MOSES, et al; attributed]. *The Holy Bible*, King James Version, Rev. Edition, Thomas Nelson, Inc., 1976.

[MOSES; attributed]. *The Sixth and Seventh Books of Moses*. Wehman Brothers, 1880. [translated from the German edition of 1865 published by Johann Scheible.]

NASSAU, Rev. Robert Hamill. *Fetichism in West Africa: Forty Years' Observation of Native Customs and Superstitions*. Charles Scribner's Sons, 1904.

PUCKETT, Newbell Niles. *Folk Beliefs of the Southern Negro*. University of North Carolina Press, 1926.

YRONWODE, Catherine and Mikhail Strabo [Sydney J. R. Steiner]. *The Art of Hoodoo Candle Magic*. Missionary Independent Spiritual Church, 2013.

YRONWODE, Catherine et al. T*he Black Folder: Personal Communications on the Mastery of Hoodoo*. Missionary Independent Spiritual Church, 2013.

YRONWODE, Catherine. *Blues Lyrics and Hoodoo*. LuckyMojo.com/blues.html. Lucky Mojo Curio Co., 1994-2018.

YRONWODE, Catherine. *Hoodoo Herb and Root Magic: A Materia Magica of African-American Conjure*. Lucky Mojo Curio Co., 2002.

YRONWODE, Catherine. *Hoodoo Rootwork Correspondence Course: A One-Year Series of Weekly Lectures in African American Conjure*. Lucky Mojo Curio Co., 2006.

YRONWODE, Catherine. *Paper in My Shoe*. Lucky Mojo Curio Co., 2015.

YRONWODE, Catherine. *Southern Spirits: Ghostly Voices from Dixie Land*. Southern-Spirits.org, 1994-2018.